In Their Words

IN THEIR WORDS

Interviews with Fourteen
Canadian Writers

by

BRUCE MEYER
and
BRIAN O'RIORDAN

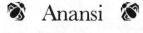 Anansi

Toronto Buffalo London Sydney

Photographs by Bruce Meyer, with special thanks to printers Zev and Adina Zemel.
Cover design by Laurel Angeloff.

Published with assistance from the Canada Council and the Ontario Arts Council, and manufactured in Canada for

House of Anansi Press Limited
35 Britain Street
Toronto, Ontario M5A 1R7

Canadian Cataloguing in Publication Data

Main entry under title:

In their words : interviews with fourteen Canadian writers

Includes bibliographies and index.
ISBN 0-88784-142-2

1. Authors, Canadian (English) - 20th century - Interviews. *I. Meyer, Bruce, 1957-
II. O'Riordan, Brian, 1953-

PS8081.I5 1984   C810'.9'0054   C84-099651-9
PR9186.2.I5 1984

---

1 2 3 4 5 / 90 89 88 87 86 85 84

Contents

Introduction

The idea for this book came about when we were taking Professor Frank Watt's University of Toronto graduate course in Contemporary Canadian Poetry. During a coffee break, one of us (neither of us can remember which) remarked that there wasn't enough recent source material in which English Canadian authors discussed what they intended their work to say, why it took shape the way it did, and why at times it was misunderstood or misinterpreted. Someone quipped that writers would never give away such secrets and talked about the numerous periodicals which publish nothing but Canadian literary criticism: "They're good but that's not exactly what we had in mind." We wanted a book where the authors set their lives and their works in the context of their own words. "Why don't you guys do something about it?" asked Professor Watt.

Several months later we both turned up on the editorial board of the student literary magazine, *The University of Toronto Review*. The editor wanted an interview with that year's Writer-in-Residence, Irving Layton, who said that he would be willing to undergo any amount of questioning as long as we brought along a bottle of Bushmill's Irish Whiskey. After the interview Layton said that he had enjoyed both the talk and the refreshments and suggested that we contact Leonard Cohen—"He has a compassionate mind." He gave us Cohen's address and three months later we were in Montreal.

And so, *In Their Words* began to take shape. For us, at least, it unfolded as a kind of treasure-hunt with one writer often suggesting the next possible subject. For instance, Timothy Findley mentioned Roo Borson as well as his television documentary on Raymond Souster. Souster reminded us that he had published the early poetry of Gwendolyn MacEwen with his Contact Press. Gwendolyn MacEwen asked if we had seen Milton Acorn, and Acorn more or less pointed the way to Purdy. In Canada, writers rarely live and work in isolation. For a nation so disparate and geographically spread out, our writers seem to need an interdependent community of independent voices. The competitions, admirations, jealousies and friendships have created a sustaining creative field, and we hope that we have captured some of that spirit in this book.

We wanted *In Their Words* to be a cross-section of English-Canadian authors. We wanted a balance of men and women, the old master and the newcomer, poets, novelists and playwrights, East and West, patriate and expatriate. We also attempted to give representation to the regional aspect of Canadian writing: Gwendolyn MacEwen, Timothy Findley and Raymond Souster are from Toronto; Dorothy Livesay, Roo Borson and Sheila Watson are associated with the West coast; Eli Mandel with the Prairies; Leonard Cohen and Irving Layton are closely identified with Montreal; Milton Acorn is a Maritimer through and through; Al Purdy is eastern Ontario's voice while James Reaney has drawn heavily on the legends and landscapes of southwestern Ontario. Brian Moore and Elizabeth Smart are Canadian writers who, though often living abroad, have retained their strong sense of identification with Canada. More than simply being tied to place, however, these authors have attempted to say something that reaches across regional and national boundaries. This is an aspect we tried to draw out through our questions.

Each interview was recorded on tape, transcribed, edited and, if requested by the writer, submitted to him or her for correction and approval. We wish to thank Professor F.W. Watt of the University of Toronto, who gave us the idea for this book, and who encouraged us and helped us at many stages along the way; Irving Layton who suggested we had the makings of a book; Mr. A. Leonard Grove for his kindness and advice; John Wilson of the League of Canadian Poets who supplied us with helpful information; Mr. and Mrs. G.H. Meyer who put up with our hours of transcription and who gave us a ride down to Ameliasburg; Margaret Meyer and Carolyn Meyer who typed several of the inverviews; Mr. and Mrs. John O'Riordan for their encouragement; James Deahl for his help and suggestions; Diane Davey and Susan Pape; Karen Mulhallen of *Descant*, Bernice Lever of *Waves* and the editors of the *University of Toronto Review* for their support in publishing several of these interviews in magazine form; James Polk, Ann Wall and Catherine Marjoribanks of Anansi for believing in this project; and above all, the writers who gave their time, support and enthusiasm. What they have said and what they continue to say is meaningful to us as a people because they speak for us in our diversity and our unity.

Bruce Meyer and Brian O'Riordan
Toronto, 1984

Irving Layton
Poet as Prophet

Layton: You're here already! Wonderful! Who asks the questions?

Interviewers: We both do.

Layton: Two of you? Not at once I hope! Ah, you've brought the glasses and you've got the Bushmills. Very efficient. Good. I'm ready for you.

Though never professing to like the academic environment, Layton, having already taught at Sir George Williams and York Universities, was now at the University of Toronto as Writer-in-Residence. The Bushmills poured, Layton folded his arms and began to speak about his Nobel Prize nominations, reminding us that his work had been translated into Hungarian, Polish, Rumanian, German, French, Portuguese, Spanish, Russian, Hebrew, Korean, and Italian.

Born in Rumania in 1912 and educated in Montreal, Irving Layton's literary career has included the 1959 Governor-General's Award for Poetry for his work, *A Red Carpet for the Sun* (1958).

Interviewers: Foreign audiences have always been more receptive to your work than Canadian ones.

Layton: I'm glad you brought that up, because sometimes it becomes a sore point with me. I say to myself: "What do you expect?" My sensibility is not Canadian, but European. I define myself as a six-thousand-year-old European. My roots go back to the Old Testament, to Moses, the Israelite slaves in Egypt, to Isaiah, Jeremiah and Amos. I have said over and over again that for me, a poet is a descendant of the prophets. As a Jew I live in both time and space—a most unusual thing for any people. No other people has had the experience the Jews have had, historically and geographically. For this reason my outlook is not Canadian.

Interviewers: It didn't come as a surprise then that it was the Italians who nominated you for the Nobel Prize in literature.

Layton: I didn't expect a nomination from the Canadians. I've been nominated by the Koreans. The same thing happened there as in Italy. A group that had been attaching themselves to me during my stay formed a committee, and when I returned to Toronto I received a telegram saying they were nominating me for the prize. I believe I'm the only writer ever to be nominated by the occident and the orient. You'll notice that the silence in this country has been loud and long and thunderous. There is no telegram to me from the Writers' Union, the Authors' Association or the League of Canadian Poets. Nothing. Now if my name was Irvine MacGregor—and I'm not saying this with any bitterness—but if this had happened to Margaret Atwood or Earle Birney, my God, can you imagine the banner headlines! I've always been a rebel and an iconoclast and always fought the literary establishment and any other establishment.

Interviewers: What is it about the Canadian psyche that creates such a narrow attitude?

Layton: You know, I recently defined a Canadian as someone who if he shoved an icicle up his asshole it wouldn't melt.

That's a Canadian for you. They don't like anyone who is too visible. They don't like shit-disturbers—Papineau, Riel or even Trudeau. They're a passive people. Remember that Canada began with two grand negations. First there was the negation of the American Revolution. The Loyalists who fled across the border were doing so because they could not accept the great ideas of Madison, Paine and Jefferson—the ideas of the separation of church and state, the concept of a republic and the other ideas of democracy. The other grand negation was in Quebec, where the French Canadians refused to accept the great ideas of the French Revolution—the ideas of Montesquieu, Rousseau and Voltaire. All these were the fathers of the enlightenment. The French Canadians turned their backs solidly on all these people and their ideas. Let's remember this about Canada. You begin with two great negations and that has influenced the Canadian psyche. So it's not surprising that Canadians don't like trouble-makers and shit-disturbers. That's in their psyche. That's in their collective unconscious. This is the phenomenon I've had to live with. This is the life I've known. I'm grateful for that kind of irritation for without it I wouldn't have written many of the poems I've written. Canadians have irritated me enough to want to write. As Frost says somewhere, a poet has a lover's quarrel with the world. Well, in a sense, I've had a lover's quarrel with my country and sometimes it is more than a lover's quarrel.

Interviewers: Nevertheless, you've continued to write about Canada and express yourself in one of its official languages. Do you see an advantage to writing in an international language such as English?

Layton: Oh, yes, definitely. Not only because English is the *lingua franca* of our times, but because it is such an expressive instrument. Lucky is the poet who knows English. Blessed and lucky.

Interviewers: Is place part of perception?

Layton: Oh yes, very much so. Wherever I've gone, I've been stimulated by the novelties I've seen all around me. The seventy-five Greek poems which I wrote could have been written only by my going to Greece and having the experiences I had.

Interviewers: In various prefaces to your works you've talked about the creative process. You talk about "The Swimmer" as the poem that set you on your path, and after it appeared you felt that you were a poet. But what about the earlier poems you wrote before "The Swimmer"? Do you remember any of them?

Layton: Oh yes. The first poem I wrote was when I was about fourteen years old. I began writing poems when I was in public school. My first poem was a very sexy one and was to my teacher, Miss Benjamin. I went on writing poems but I never could think of myself as a poet. For me, in those days, a poet had to be an Englishman or he had to be dead. I never knew there were Canadian poets. I studied Byron, Shelley and Shakespeare and even when I went on to Baron Byng High School we didn't study Canadian poets. It was a kind of brainwashing. It never occurred to me, a Canadian Jew living in Montreal, that I could be a poet. Even when I was writing at McGill, I never thought of myself as a poet.

Interviewers: Did you feel that a poet had to be educated?

Layton: That unfortunate notion never entered my mind.

Interviewers: Nevertheless, you did go to university.

Layton: Yes, and I'm very grateful that I did. I could not have achieved what I have achieved without going. Without destroying my energies, it gave me the necessary background for which I will always be grateful. University gave me the opportunity to write. That's when I first encountered Louis Dudek. His poems, along with mine, appeared in *The McGill Daily.* I can't recall who made the first advance but we managed to meet and out of the first collaboration came *First*

Statement with John Sutherland. That was the beginning of modern poetry in Canada.

Interviewers: What do you remember about the "Montreal Group" that was focused around McGill?

Layton: I got out of the army in 1943 when they realized I was never going to make it as an artillery officer. I received an honourable discharge. I had met John Sutherland's sister, Betty, and had fallen in love with her. Sutherland was just starting *First Statement* and he invited me to join the editorial board with Louis Dudek. We formed the nucleus of *First Statement*. What was great about that period was that there was also *Preview*, the rival magazine, run by a very strange and very gifted man, Patrick Anderson. Anderson was an expatriate from England who had a knowledge of Spender, Dylan Thomas and Auden. We knew little or nothing about these poets. Anderson was also influenced by Rilke, of whom we knew nothing either. Frank Scott, A.M. Klein, A.J.M. Smith, and P.K. Page at *Preview* were all being influenced by the British while we at *First Statement* were influenced by the Americans, Walt Whitman, William Carlos Williams, e.e. cummings and Wallace Stevens. These two great influences came together and resulted in a very stimulating rivalry. We were watching each other very carefully like runners looking back to see if anyone was catching up with us. It was an intense and glorious and tremendously creative time. Blessed to have been alive then.

Interviewers: Louis Dudek once said that Montreal was the shaping influence on the poetry of the nation.

Layton: There's no question about it. Montreal poetry was the shaping influence. People are still living off the tremendous energy of that time. Montreal is still for me the important centre of Canadian poetry.

Interviewers: What influence did A.M. Klein have on you?

Layton: Little, in the poetic sense. Klein was important to me because (a) he was a poet, and (b) he was surviving at a time when if you were a poet you kept it secret. Like masturbation—you enjoyed it but didn't tell anyone about it. In Klein there was a visible poet and a dedicated one. He taught me Latin and the text was Virgil, Book Two. I remember Klein's thunderous vocables, and I'll never forget the marvellous music and his delight in poetic sound. So that was the great influence. But we disagreed. He was a believing Jew but not an orthodox one. I had turned my back on that. The good Father for me had not existed for some time, not since he suffocated my first love, which was a cat, in a fire. I lost faith in Him. Then Klein and I disagreed on politics, on poetry, and on many other things. But he wrote the best review of my first book, *Here and Now*. If you really want to see how someone can be perceptive, read the review he wrote of my work back in 1945 and compare it with what has been written since. It is incredible. He said I was a Jewish poet, not in the sense of the subject matter and themes, but in outlook and sensibility.

Interviewers: Louis Dudek was Pound's assistant for a while . . .

Layton: Louis and I began to disagree. He went to New York and came back hot-gospelling Pound. To me Pound was a bit of a bore. He had not made the transmutation from the base metal into the gold of poetry. He has some marvellous lyrics, but he's not a major poet. Pound is nowhere near a Dante or a Wordsworth or a Milton. He was a minor poet, who like the frog in the fable blew himself up into a big girth. What will remain of Pound will be the perfect lyrics he has written. I don't think the *Cantos* is a successful epic.

Interviewers: In the context of what you've just said, do you see the function of myth in poetry as more than a form of echoing—as a translation of old substance through new experience?

Layton: Oh certainly. A good poet does that. The basic thing about a good poet is his experience and what he does with it.

You can use the Bible or Homeric myth, but the transformation comes only with your personality. That is what transmutes the metal into gold. What we are interested in is the individual voice of the poet. The poetic voice means that the poet knows consciously or unconsciously that we and he are all travellers on this planet. We have a journey and it is the poet who is telling us what the journey means to him. He hopes that what has happened to him will benefit others when it is put down in poetry.

Interviewers: In that context, how has your early life shaped your ability to write?

Layton: That's any poet's capital. Rilke said that the poet's childhood is the most important part of his life and thereafter he is always trying to find its meaning. The poet is searching in the ashes of his past life and the ashes of his memory for the meanings hidden in those ashes. This is the poetic quest—the search for meaning. What does it mean? What does the first sexual encounter mean? What did it mean when my Cousin Fanny, who was staying at my house and who was five years older than myself but frustrated and luscious and beautiful— what did it mean when she began to play with me? Me, an orthodox boy brought up with a puritanical fear of sex, etc.? What did it mean when my beloved kitten died in a fire? What did it mean? Where was God? And I asked that question again and again—where was God? Where was God when the Jews were herded into Auschwitz? It is always with increased itensity and awareness that you keep coming back to the questions of sex, religion and death.

I had my first encounter with sex at a very early age because of Cousin Fanny. I had my first encounter with death at the age of ten or eleven when my brother Abraham died of T.B. He was a very tall man—we were runts by comparison. His body was washed in the house and made ready for the coffin. I happened to find myself on the banister outside the room where my brother's body was being put into the coffin and they were trying to get his long body into this short coffin.

There were two men standing at the end where his head was and they pressed the head down and his feet came out at the other end. Two men at the other end pressed his feet down and the head came up. This went on for several minutes. Can you imagine a child watching that? This ludicrous, comical, grotesque thing happening? This is why I called the poem about the incident "Seesaw". Someone who has that experience at the age of ten and a half—it is something that affects him for the rest of his life. His attitude towards life and death is going to be different. That was my first experience with death, which I have explored in poem after poem.

And then you have religion. My father was an orthodox Jew and I don't know whether you are familiar with the quaint customs that Jews observe on the Sabbath, but you are not supposed to switch on any lights. You can't even whistle. One Sabbath when I was about nine years old, I said: "Will God really strike me dead if I turn on the lights now? He must have something more important on his mind than that." I remember going back and forth, tempted to turn on the light but feeling I was risking death if I did. I went ahead and turned on the switch and when the light came on I thought it was lightning and I fell back against the wall sure I had been struck. But nothing happened. That was my first defiance of orthodoxy. That has been with me in different forms right up until now. So, yes, of course, you carry these things with you. First experiences are the matrix, the idea, the feeling, and, above all, the sensation.

Interviewers: Why do people avoid confronting the reality of death?

Layton: It is the one invasion into our ego that is so final, so complete and unanswerable. If somebody kicks you in the belly you can fight back. If someone insults you or slaps your face you can fight back. How do you fight back against death? Death says you're nothing, that you and all your accomplishments are nothing. Life is struggle. It is the constant struggle against that final insult of death. Some of us give up one way or another. The artist can never come to terms with death. That's what makes him an artist. That's the whole secret. The enemy is death and poets feel it in their bones. They write about sex and death and they are two sides of the same coin. With young poets I always look to see if they have any poems about fucking, about death. If they don't, they're not poets.

Interviewers: What happens when a poet stops writing or pauses in his career?

Layton: Once you break that nerve, once you rupture that connection you can't bring it together again. Once you lose that faith you can't get it back again—the poetry. It was Pushkin who said that the poem is a kiss that the poet gives to the world. In the beginning was the word. That's what makes us human. That's what brings us together. It's the language. It's the word. That's what poetry and the poet are all about. The poet is the great guardian of that mystery and he must always remember that and must always be true to that no matter how onerous the burden may be.

Interviewers: Is your friend Leonard Cohen someone who has lost faith? Will he ever write poetry again?

Layton: No, I don't think he will write poetry again. But I know that presently he is working on a mini-musicale.

Interviewers: Over the years you've had a lot of contact with him. Didn't you even collaborate with him on a number of plays?

Layton: That's right! How do you know this? Leonard and I collaborated on them twenty years ago. One of them, *A Man Was Killed*, was produced twice. Leonard was living in Montreal at the time and we used to meet every day and work on the plays. We wrote together, something like six or seven plays. They're on file at the University of Toronto, and several people have looked at them and said they're good. But the CBC, being what it is, gave us no encouragement at all. We were working completely in the blind. We didn't have any idea at all of technique or anything. My God, if they'd sent us down anyone to point out elementary things or given us any encouragement at all we'd have gone on to write fine things. I'll never forgive the CBC for that. They lost two very talented dramatists.

Interviewers: Are you still in contact with Cohen?

Layton: We've been good friends for a quarter of a century. He claims I kicked open the doors for him, which I did for a whole generation. I broke down all the literary taboos. You must remember that when I began to write no Canadian went to the bathroom or fucked.

Interviewers: Was that because people set poetry above the other arts?

Layton: No. It was the sensibility of the time and the gentility that I have been battling since I first began to write. Poetry was supposed to deal only with nice things. You spoke of the stars, the moon and flowers. You couldn't say 'even'; you were supposed to say 'e'en'. The deal was that poetry dealt only with beautiful things. You didn't say anything that was ugly or disgusting or talk about ash-cans or whorehouses. The fact that I saw whorehouses in my neighbourhood on De Bullion Street didn't matter. You weren't supposed to write about these things. That was the sensibility I was batting my head against at that time. The poets that came later didn't have to do that and didn't have to fight for a broadened perspective. You know in my new book, *The Gucci Bag*, my symbol for the bourgeois world, the world of materialism, what I'm saying is the poet and the poet alone is the permanent opposition. It is not the communists, or trotskyists, or socialists. It is only the poet. That is to say the prophets—the Isaiahs, the Ezekiels, the Jesuses that form the permanent opposition. And that's what the book is about.

Interviewers: Every poet has certain poetic criteria and standards. What are yours?

Layton: I don't know. I like wisdom. I like passion. I like clarity. I like to see a man articulating what life is all about. I expect my poet to be a very profound, experienced and passionate individual. My definition for genius is wisdom and passion. That's what I look for in a poem. I like the later Yeats because he has the wisdom, and he's looked at history and the world while at the same time he's still a passionate old man. With wisdom comes a diminution of passion and with passion, wisdom flies out the window. Genius is being able to corral both of them at once. That's what I look for in poetry.

Interviewers: Do you feel that by speaking out on human rights, in favour of life, that there won't be another Buchenwald, another Kampuchea, another Armenia?

Layton: What other faith is there? The faith of the poet is the only thing. By giving up you're submitting to oppression. We don't throw dice with words. If you're a poet you go ahead. If you're a prophet, you go ahead and say what has to be said even though you know, like Jeremiah, you're going to be cast into a pit or if you're a Jesus you're going to be crucified or burned at the stake like Bruno. Right? That's what it means to be a human being. You don't ask whether you're going to be successful or not. That's for emperors, captains, kings and generals. It is not for poets. You go on doing it. You have to speak the word, hoping that eventually you'll catch fire and people's minds and lives and spirits will be changed.

Interviewers: You've always been someone who's been outspoken politically. In recent years you've written about human rights and the holocaust. You've generally been thought of as on the left of the political spectrum. Many leftists, however, have criticized you for your support of American involvement in Viet Nam, Nixon's bombing of Cambodia and the imposition of the War Measures Act. How do you answer these criticisms?

Layton: I resent labelling, but yes you could say I've been a leftist sympathizer. In fact I was once a member of a Commu-

nist cell in Halifax. But I tore up my card after Russia signed
the non-aggression pact with Hitler and the party embraced
'social fascism' and tried to sell me on the idea that there was
no difference between fascism and democracy. This is sheer
idiocy. From that point on I began to attack the Soviet
Union. I began to attack Communism because I saw the true
face of Communism. It didn't make me a right-winger and it
didn't make me a fascist. I don't believe in any kind of
rehearsed knee-jerking. I distrust all labels, ideologies and all
ideologues. In regard to Viet Nam, I am proud of my record.
At the time I wrote that it was a mistake for the United States
to go into the war and I said this as early as 1955. But it was
not ethically wrong for the United States to support the
independence of South Viet Nam, and I hold to that position.
I am proud of having said this at a time when all the knee-
jerking liberal left-wingers and progressives were telling me
that Uncle HoHo was an agrarian reformer and that he loved
children and mankind. The "boat people" and what has
happened in Viet Nam have vindicated me completely.
Those who criticized me do not have the gall to look me in the
eye. I told them that, since I had had experience with real
Communists and they had not, they were talking plain bullshit. They also refused to believe me when I told them that
this was the Russians' war and not the war of the Vietnamese.
The Soviet Union is playing a marvellously clever game of
geo-politics.

I also feel that I have been vindicated in terms of my
support of the War Measures Act. I felt at the time that
Trudeau knew more than he was willing to tell, that the
threat was bigger and more serious than we knew. We now
see that the P.Q. have links with the P.L.O. They invite them
to their conventions and Jacques Rose, a convicted terrorist,
gets a standing ovation at the meeting. When the government
smashed the F.L.Q. in 1971 the terrorists and their sympa-
thizers went underground. The F.L.Q. were bringing the
province to the edge of chaos but they realized after 1971 they
had to do it by legal means. They infiltrated the P.Q. and

decided to try and take power by legal, rather than violent, means. But now they have been exposed. They got excited when they saw themselves on the verge of achieving separation. They have tipped their hand and we see them for what they really are. And so once again I feel that I am completely vindicated.

What we must not forget is that we are facing a wily, tough and resilient enemy in the Russians. They will stop at nothing to achieve their ends. Unless the West wakes up to this serious danger, our civilization will slide down into ignominious defeat. All these international terrorist organizations are controlled and bankrolled by the Soviet Union. What they're doing is posing the question: Are we willing to fight for freedom? What they've done to Poland they'll do to any other country. They're always finding people to aid them in suppression. People lust for power almost as much as poets crave and protect their freedom. Unless we get that message we're lost. That's what a prophet must do—make that message heard and valued. It is the essential practice of the prophet's vision.

Interviewers: Earlier you defined the role of the poet as a prophet. What is a prophet?

Layton: The prophet is someone who addresses himself to the moral, the psychological, the social and political dilemmas of his time. That's the prophet. He can see and sense because his vision penetrates into the souls of people, how they're going to handle these problems and see whether they're going to behave with valour and intelligence and confront these problems as human beings, with dignity and intelligence. That's how I see the prophet. He spots the threats to the human spirit. I exalt the human spirit above all. Man is a strange animal. He's an animal to begin with, but he's a very peculiar animal because he craves dignity, exhibits reason, loves beauty, and has a conscience. But above all, he's creative. The grandest metaphor of all time is that God made Man in His own image. It is a beautiful way of saying that Man is the only creative creature in the whole universe. For me that's fundamental. When I look at a child in a crib, when I see little children and they manifest right away that wonderful vitality and that marvellous curiosity, my faith in mankind is renewed. I can barely keep back tears when I see little children and what they do and their games and inventiveness, their vitality and curiosity. That's my vision. That's my poet's vision. This is what the poet knows about the human being. This is what he wants to preserve and protect against the Stalins, the Hitlers, the Castros and all the others who want to reduce human beings to automatons. It is the waywardness and the dignity of the human being that I uphold and fight for. Both poet and prophet fight for this. That's what a prophet is all about.

Leonard Cohen
Working for the World to Come

We rang the buzzer on the front door. No answering voices, no footsteps were heard. Suddenly the bolt lifted on the lock and the door apparently opened by itself. "Hello?" "C'mon up," a voice called from the top of the stairs. We crouched down in order to look up the stairs that were directly in front of us. At the top of the flight stood Leonard Cohen peering down, holding a long string which was connected to the lock on the door. Another string worked the door shut.

Interviewers: You work the door like a kite?

Cohen: Yeah. It's fun.

It was a cold mid-winter's afternoon and we were at Leonard Cohen's Montreal duplex-studio. He took our coats and led us into the kitchen where we sat down at an old walnut dining room table. The walls of the apartment were white. Simplicity of form and colour dominated the place. In a corner of the kitchen there was a waterheater with a large bust of Irving Layton sitting on top of it. Next to the door an electric socket protruded from the wall and on top rested another Layton icon—a small pen and ink profile. We chatted for a while and then took some photographs in the bedroom and the living-room. On the living-room wall the only adornment, a painting of an unidentified female saint, stood out against the white surface.

The buzzer rang. "That's Mort with the schnapps," said Cohen. In walked Montreal artist, Morton Rosengarten, and we all went into the kitchen where after a few glasses of schnapps, Cohen said: "Let's do it."

Leonard Cohen was born in Montreal in 1934 and educated at McGill and Columbia. He won, but declined to accept, the 1968 Governor-General's Award for Poetry for *Selected Poems 1956-1968*.

Interviewers: What are you working on now? We've heard it described as a mini-musicale?

Cohen: I'm in the midst of a new record and a new book of poems but I've also been working on an opera with Montreal composer Lewis Furey. It could be described as a demotic opera. In other words, it's an opera, but it's not a rock opera. It's an opera in the sense that the music is quite complex and it's not based on two-four or four-four rhythms like a rock opera. The difference is that it's colloquial or demotic. It's not for trained voices. It has the formality of an opera, with about an hour and a half of music.

Interviewers: Is it being taped or done live?

Cohen: Our original concept was a video tape for television—a video disc. It could be adapted for stage, but it isn't far enough along. The possibilities of production will determine it's final form.

Interviewers: When will it appear?

Cohen: Well, it's ready now and it's just a matter of finding a channel for it.

Interviewers: Is it designed for a Canadian, or an international market?

Cohen: Well, it wasn't designed with any borders in mind. I think it could play anywhere. We'd like to put it on in Canada and have it as one of the first productions of the private pay-television apparatus. I think that would be appropriate.

Interviewers: What will the text be like?

Cohen: The lyrics are mostly in Spenserian stanzas. There are three or four hundred lines of verse in it, mostly in Spenserian stanza.

Interviewers: Is there a story behind it?

Cohen: It resembles the Faust story.

Interviewers: But it's not the Faust story?

Cohen: No. It's not the Faust story. I think the story is about as important as the story is in an opera, which means it isn't terribly important. Mostly in an opera the action is conveyed musically. You have people singing lines like: "Pass the butter." Then: "No, I'll have the salt." (Laughter.) And it's all in Spenserian stanzas.

Interviewers: That's an interesting extension of the songs because songs sometimes can convey much more meaning than poetry. You once said that songs are not as pedagogical.

Cohen: I don't think I ever set up a conflict or comparison between songs and poetry. It's just a different mode. There is something about reading lines on a page which is very powerful. Hearing something also has its powers. I wouldn't set up a conflict between forms.

Interviewers: Do you think there is any strategy involved in employing a video cassette at a time when popular culture is becoming increasingly more visually oriented?

Cohen: I've never had a strategy. To me it was perfectly natural that my work would penetrate and find an audience in the popular culture. We live in a popular culture and I think you can approach it in any way you want. I think it's important not to let it tyrannize you. I don't think we're completely creatures of that culture and neither are we creatures of our own personal culture. We're continually moving back and forth between those two areas. I never had a strategy because I never felt alien from popular culture. You just set the thing up in the way you can handle it. I don't have the kind of mind to do anything else. I think Irving Layton once described my mind as "unblemished by a single idea." I never had a plan. I had a certain kind of faith although I would never have given that word to it. If the work was good enough or, more specifically, if the work was *appropriate* to move into the world, it would move into the world. There are certain kinds of work that move into the world appropriately and certain kinds of work that stay with you. You don't develop any kind of chip on your shoulder because that kind of work doesn't move out or gain hundreds of admirers. I have a clear idea of the process, of a song say, in the popular realm. The world can use certain kinds of work at certain times and at certain times it can't. You can't develop an ideology about the world or about yourself in regard to how your work is accepted. You just do what you have to do to satisfy a certain hunger or loneliness, in order to make contact with the world. There is a tradition of contact that has been going on for thousands of years. It's not just your solitary effort in the matter but generations of men before you who have done the same thing and have tended to connect in the same kind of way. So that tradition is there. You can lean on it and be encouraged by it and sustained by it.

Interviewers: Do you think that you're getting back closer to the roots of poetry as it was probably originally sung?

Cohen: I'm not sure about that—whether it was originally sung. That's one of the superstitions we have to make us anxious about what we're doing. I'm not sure whether it was originally sung ... or whispered.

Interviewers: On your last album, *Recent Songs*, there was a different sound and a wider range than with some of the other albums. You weren't quite as angry or self-deprecating. Is that a fair reading of it?

Cohen: That's grossly unfair. (Laughter.) That's hard to say from the outside, because I never have the sense of the luxury of choice. Songs come from a certain endeavour and you surround them with the kind of accompaniment that they require. So the thing is not done objectively, it's done organically. It emerges just the way it is.

Interviewers: You don't set out to do that?

Cohen: Yeah.

Interviewers: On your last album you had a song "Un Canadien Errant" with a mariachi band as back-up musicians. It emerged sounding like a very Latin tune rather than a Québécois folksong.

Cohen: I thought the resonances that were developed through that kind of treatment were quite interesting and humorous, because you have a Jew singing a French-Canadian song with a Mexican band. So it really does become a statement of exile.

Interviewers: Is there any reason why you left out the last verse?

Cohen: I never knew the last verse too well. How does it go?

Interviewers: Something like: "Even though I die, my Canada, I will expire or languish with your name forever with me— my dear Canada."

Cohen: I don't think I ever used to sing that. I hadn't sung that song for years and years. What were the French words?

Interviewers: "Non mais on expirant, O mon cher Canada, Mon regard languissant, Vers toi se portera."

Cohen: (Pause.) I remember vaguely hearing those. I never learned those, and the song seemed to work with two verses and instrumental and final verse.

Interviewers: Do you see French-Canadians in the context of that song? Was that song directed specifically at them?

Cohen: The complexities of singing that song are enormous. I think it would take volumes to unfold. It just has a certain irony, humour and poignancy in the way it was done, because in a certain sense, we—the English-speaking Canadians in Montreal—are the exiles. The song turns around and has harmonics that are quite interesting.

Interviewers: You dedicated the album *Recent Songs* to Irving Layton. What sort of relationship do you have with him?

Cohen: It's more a friendship which involves mutual respect. We're friends, and fortunately we also happen to like each other's work. I can't really determine any literary characteristics to the friendship. He's just a guy I like. He's a guy who likes me. We've been friends for twenty-five years. I think a lot of stuff has rubbed off both ways. I've never studied his work to see if there have been influences on my work. There was a great deal of his work I didn't understand until I got older. A lot of his work about marriage and that sort of thing I didn't understand until I was married. I think there are positions that have migrated back and forth between us. I write from a more liturgical Jewish background which I was closer to. He's using a cultural background. I think that still is the case. Irving sees the Jewish people with a kind of destiny in the world, which I also see. But the approaches are different. It would be a good study to look for mutual influences. There is something to be examined there.

Interviewers: You've also been associated with Louis Dudek over the years. He brought out your first book from Contact Press.

Cohen: I'm fond of Louis Dudek, but I don't think he's fond of me. I think he feels I've sold out to Mammon and took a wrong turning somewhere. I think he considers me less pure than I might be. His view is much like that of Ezra Pound, that the world is irrevocably corrupt—a very Manichean view, where you have the artists on one side, who are very pure, and on the other side you have the world which is Satanic and you don't make an accommodation with the world. It's a very Christian idea. I don't think the world is stained irrevocably. I don't buy this view. I don't think the purity of the artist is concerned with those matters. There is such a thing as integrity and purity but I don't think it rests on those kinds of activity. I think that we have to recognize that in 'the world' there are certain activities, publications like *Playboy* and *Esquire*, and they too have certain standards of craftsmanship. There are certain standards of excellence that operate in the world that are valuable for any artist. There is also the danger that if you isolate yourself in a certain artistic circle, an artistic community or milieu, that you will not even be satisfying the operative standards of excellence which pertain in the world at large.

Interviewers: What is the only essential ground-rule?

Cohen: I think that excellence is the only standard. There's all kinds of other matters like making a living and freedom from having to satisfy whatever regulations pertain to the artistic circle, which are often very tyrannical. I never felt my work needed any label or refuge.

Interviewers: There's a woodcut on the cover of *Death of a Lady's Man* and also on the sleeve of the album *New Skin for the Old Ceremony* which is taken from a book by Jung. Has Jung been an influence on you?

Cohen: I don't know Jung's work that well, but I've kept his books as references throughout the years. I know the general Jungian principles. I more or less came to Jung through oriental studies. He'd written some prefaces to the *I Ching* and also *The Secret of the Golden Flower.* As a western scientist, his appreciation of the Oriental psychology and Oriental psychical anatomy—mysticism, whatever that means—dissolved the western view that their psychology was mystical. He saw systematically a diagram of the psyche. It was valid. That kind of view developed in the West in the Forties where we had a radical change in our perception of their work. I think Jung probably led in that re-evaluation of Oriental methodology. It's the science of the orient. It's not mysticism. The word mysticism is used in a somewhat pejorative sense. The point Jung makes in all his prefaces is that these things are pragmatic, that they refer to the mechanics of the psyche and can be properly studied. He de-mystified the work that the orientals had done.

Interviewers: Were you trying to use Jungian psychology and techniques in *Death of a Lady's Man?*

Cohen: I don't really remember what the premise of the book was because, as I said, I don't write from a position of luxury. I write from a position of scraping the bottom of the barrel. I don't really know what that book was about. As I say in one of the paragraphs "my work is alive." Wherever you can go to find those mechanics that produce a living thing, that is where I have to go, because I'm not at a banquet table where I can pick and choose from all the delicacies. You go to the place that gives you those elements that can produce something that is alive.

Interviewers: So writing *Death of a Lady's Man* wasn't the kind of draining or purifying experience that *Beautiful Losers* was.

Cohen: I think *Beautiful Losers* was the same thing. You always try to do your best.

Interviewers: With what is at hand at the time?

Cohen: Yes. Whatever scraps, shards you have at your disposal.

Interviewers: What did you mean when you said that *The Favourite Game* was a third novel and not a first?

Cohen: I had written a first novel, *The Ballet of Lepers*, and had written a lot of short stories and long pieces and I completely overhauled the various versions of *The Favourite Game*. There is another *Favourite Game* that exists in the Thomas Fisher Library at the University of Toronto which is radically different from the one I published. I had done at least four versions of *The Favourite Game* so by the time the final novel came out it wasn't a first novel.

Interviewers: Montreal has played a major role in your novels. Have you deliberately set out to render the life of the city or was the sense of the city just incidentally in the work?

Cohen: I was just talking to a girl—Gail Scott—who is writing a book that's trying to give you a sense of the city, like Joyce's *Dubliners*—that makes the city come alive. No, I never began with an intention to render the life of the city. I began with hunger. An appetite. I never believed I had to justify the city because I was in the city and that this city, Montreal, was the "Jerusalem of the North," that this was a holy city. The spirit was somehow invigorated here. It was illuminated. We were here already. I didn't have to invoke it.

Interviewers: So once again, it's just the material at hand.

Cohen: Mostly, that's it. If there is an aesthetic, you go where you go to feel alive.

Interviewers: You wrote an unpublished story, "The Juke Box Heart" . . .

Cohen: What was that about? That's a great title!

Interviewers: In it you wrote of growing up to approximate a thirteen-year old's romantic dream of the outsider, the exile, the private-eye figure who walks dark, wet streets late at night with a hat pulled down over one eye.

Cohen: No recollection of that at all. (Laughter.) Great story. I mean not the slightest recollection.

Interviewers: Does the detective figure attract you—Sam Spade, etc.?

Cohen: Well, I've always liked raincoats.

Interviewers: Particularly blue ones. Do you still have one?

Cohen: Yes. I'll put it on. (Puts on raincoat.) How about a picture under the bare lightbulb?

Interviewers: I think you've answered our question about whether one grows up to approximate one's thirteen-year old fantasies.

Cohen: I'm glad you guys are getting down to the important stuff.

Interviewers: Has any pop-romantic figure, such as Bogart, influenced you?

Cohen: I've never been particularly influenced by anything that's going down.

Interviewers: In the Sixties you were quite into pop culture.

Cohen: I always was.

Interviewers: Do you like pop culture?

Cohen: Sure. When it's good. I don't feel separated from it. I listen to radio a good deal. I have my views as to whether the music is good and is speaking to me, but I certainly recognize that I'm part of it. I never felt "that's going on and I'm not with it." I always felt it was mine and I always felt it was good and there's always something good happening in that realm at all times.

Interviewers: Do you see yourself as being type-cast as a Sixties figure? Has it been a problem for you?

Cohen: I don't think it's a problem. I think it's certainly true. Certainly here in Canada.

Interviewers: Do you see Canada as developing a certain mythos? I'm speaking specifically of Kateri Tekakwitha, who has just been beatified.

Cohen: I did a lot for that girl. I was very gratified when someone sent me an Italian newspaper on the day she was beatified and it had an excerpt in Italian from *Beautiful Losers*. I did love the woman.

Interviewers: Do you see yourself as the advocate for that saint?

Cohen: Oh, I'm behind her all the way. I'd like to see her advance into every heart. (Laughter.)

Interviewers: Has the Christian mythos been a creative force for you?

Cohen: I love Christ. I see Christianity as the world historic mission of certain ideas that the Jews developed. Christianity is a mighty movement, and that is the way those ideas penetrated the world. Christianity is the missionary arm of Judaism. As Maimonides said, "We're all working for the world to come."

Interviewers: Do you have any vision of that world to come?

Cohen: No, except that one inhabits it from time to time. You fall out of it and then climb back into it.

Interviewers: What has it been like when you've been in it?

Cohen: Wonderful. It's almost like this one.

Interviewers: It has schnapps and everything. (Laughter.) You said once that what was lacking in Judaism now is the prophet's vision—that the prophet and the prophetic vision had been down-graded in Judaism and all that was left was the priests.

Cohen: I said that?

Interviewers: Yes, and it caused quite a commotion at the time. It was in a speech before the Symposium on the Future of Judaism in 1964.

Cohen: I went that far?

Interviewers: And you said a lot worse but far be it from us to bring all that up. (Laughter.)

Cohen: I think at the time I said that I was simply unaware of what the Jewish tradition was. I think that within our tradition there have been various attempts to understand Christianity and make an accommodation with the figure of

Christ. I was unaware of Maimonides' statement at the time. Christ and Mohammed were toilers in the vineyard. Based on ignorance and some distorted views of the Jewish tradition, I said those things. My studies now indicate that Judaism is now not lacking in the vision of the prophet.

Interviewers: Have you visited Israel?

Cohen: Yes, I was there under many circumstances: as a tourist, as a volunteer in the armed forces and as a performer. I think it is a very great country, probably the most democratic country in the world. It's alive.

Interviewers: How does Jerusalem compare to Montreal?

Cohen: They've got a long way to go. (Laughter.)

Interviewers: How do you feel when academics categorize your work?

Cohen: You know, it just depends on the academic. Someone like Dennis Lee—I'd be hard-pressed to call him an academic. Some men arise and are generous and don't have an ideology to lean on. It doesn't matter to Dennis Lee why *Beautiful Losers* came about, whether or not it was my pitch to hit the bestseller lists, or a private vision, or whether it compromises the idea of artistic purity. Those things are irrelevant to a man like Dennis Lee. Dennis Lee understands that the work arises and he has to confront it. That to my mind is the mark of a high spirit and a high critical process.

Interviewers: You've said that your work could survive regardless of what form it eventually took. Was there any particular point where you said, "I know this is good, regardless, and is something that is artistic and can endure?"

Cohen: I never had a landmark in my mind. I never really was touched by those concerns. It was a matter of the work and wherever it would go, there it would go. I had a certain kind of confidence that part of it would move out—that part of it would leave the page and touch other hearts.

Interviewers: You were in Havana during the Bay of Pigs fiasco and wrote a poem, "The Only Canadian Tourist in Havana Turns His Thoughts Homeward..." Why did you go down there?

Cohen: I don't know.

Interviewers: You seem to have walked into several revolutions. Greece before the Colonels took over, Ethiopia...

Cohen: Yeah, I've been into a few of those places. I've actually stumbled into my share of revolutions, I guess.

Interviewers: Was it purely coincidental, or...

Cohen: I guess there might be some unseen hand at work.

Interviewers: Politically, as an English writer living in Quebec with roots here, how have you been affected by the advent of a Separatist government?

Cohen: Seems very familiar to me. I don't feel anything has happened. I think this was always happening and that this has always been the spirit of the province. It moves, it changes continually. We're in a period now where the majority of the people are asserting their own sense of themselves. It will intensify and de-intensify depending on what the conditions are. It seems to be natural and appropriate. I can't get myself revved-up about it.

Interviewers: That last line in the Havana poem—do you think that you or anyone else has broken that "stoney silence on the Seaway"?

Cohen: I think everybody has broken it. I don't quite know what I meant by that line. I think that whatever we call this thing, Canada, that it's one of the best places in the world. It's our ambiguities about it that make it great. Those ambiguities about it create all kinds of loopholes wherein we can operate with a great deal of freedom. I don't have an aggressive view of Canada. I have a very warm feeling about this country.

Interviewers: Is that why you come back so often?

Cohen: Yeah.

Interviewers: In the 1965 film *Ladies and Gentlemen, Mr. Leonard Cohen* you were painted as a sort of rebel. Do you see yourself in those terms?

Cohen: Those are other people's labels. You indulge in fantasies about who you are and what you're doing and what your work is worth. You move from a position of significance or insignificance. You move back and forth between those poles in terms of what you are and what you do.

Interviewers: You once said that the job of the poet is to make the reader say, "This is what I am." Do you still see that role for yourself as the 'evocateur' of yourself in other people, to make them recognize who they are? Is that still there?

Cohen: It's not a bad statement. It isn't something I'd say now but it isn't something I'd repudiate. I think the idea of recognizing your true self vivifies all selves.

Interviewers: In terms of your music, was there any deliberate decision on your part not to tour Canada?

Cohen: I don't know how that came about. I feel I should tour Canada. The mechanics of the operation are a little more difficult for me and that involves relationships with the record company, with the media and eventually comes down to my livelihood since it's a tremendous effort to tour. I tend to tour in those places where the audience is already there, and the distance between cities is short—for instance, France. When I meet people in Canada they say, "Are you still singing, I haven't heard you in a long time?" Much of that is my fault. I haven't really devoted any time to Canadian audiences and there is an audience in Europe that is aware of what I do. When I get around to touring, and the tremendous effort that is involved in touring, I tend to go to those places where it's 'cooking'.

Interviewers: You were recently in Australia. How were the audiences there?

Cohen: Australia is a wonderful country. Sometimes I think if I was twenty years old I'd go there. It's very beautiful. It's an island in the South Pacific where everybody speaks English and they have electricity. (Laughter.) I was surprised with the audiences and the familiarity with my work.

Interviewers: Death of a Lady's Man was tremendously popular in England.

Cohen: Yeah, it did okay there. Different segments of the work connect with different countries.

Interviewers: If you won the Governor-General's Award today, would you turn it down as you did in 1969?

Cohen: I think they should give it to me anyways and let me decide. I think I would accept it now. I feel I would want to affirm Canada.

Interviewers: How important is privacy and elusiveness?

Cohen: I wish you guys would go immediately! No really, in a very pedestrian way, you have to have a lot of time to yourself or else you're not going to do anything. I think it does encourage a certain ruthlessness in your character just to clear away the time that you need to satisfy your hunger to blacken pages. You've got to be quite severe with yourself and with your family.

Interviewers: This is a bit like asking you "Is professional wrestling fixed" ....

Cohen: That's a theological question.

Interviewers: You once said that "the Romantic Movement was the last attempt of men to disguise what they'd always known about women." What have you always known about women?

Cohen: They drive me crazy!

Interviewers: Do you have any heroes? What do you consider a hero?

Cohen: What I consider a hero is a guy who goes to work every day and supports his family. The ordinary guy. I think to hold it together nowadays is a heroic enterprise.

Interviewers: How do you want to be remembered?

Cohen: Uh, how about 'He's a great guy'?

Interviewers: Is that it?

Cohen: No. I haven't said my last word. I'm still scratching away.

Timothy Findley
The Marvel of Reality

As we walked along Yorkville Avenue from the Library to the hotel, our conversation drifted to the topic of guns. Something bizarre caught Timothy Findley's eye and he stopped abruptly. "Look at that. Isn't it marvellous?" On a brick wall someone had spray-painted the silhouette of a hand-gun and backgrounded the image with a violent splatter of red paint.

When we arrived at the hotel, Findley unwound a green scarf which he always wears at readings. It was initialled "H.S.M." for Hugh Selwyn Mauberley, the wandering novelist/protagonist of Findley's recent work, *Famous Last Words*.

The interview was conducted, appropriately enough, in one of Toronto's grand hotels, The Four Seasons on Avenue Road. As Findley sat, surrounded by silver and Chippendale, on a wicker lounge in the hotel's tea-room, he glanced nostalgically out onto the street. "I used to live in a house on that corner many years ago. This city fascinates me, so much changes, so much stays the same."

Findley's novel, *The Wars*, won him the Governor-General's Award, and was turned into a feature length film, directed by Robin Phillips. Timothy Findley was born in Toronto in 1930 and received his education there before leaving school to devote himself to acting. As well as writing fiction he has worked on television and film scripts and was Playwright-in-Residence at the National Arts Centre in Ottawa.

Interviewers: In *Famous Last Words*, you employ the mode of what might be called historical fiction or fictionalized history, which you also used in *The Wars*. What were the difficulties and the advantages of employing such a mode? How do you determine how to treat characters like the Duke and Duchess of Windsor, Ezra Pound, Sir Harry Oakes, etc.?

Findley: My first part of the answer has to be that you don't put them in unless there's something that attracts you to them, something about the aura, or the story, or whatever, that draws you to them as people. It's not enough to want them in the plot and then, for instance, throw in the Duke and Duchess of Windsor. You've got to really want to know them as people. The thing that was interesting, particularly with Wallis (the Duchess) was the more I wrote about her the more she became mine. Something about her seemed to be inside me, to come from inside. There's no question all of this comes from inside you.

Interviewers: It's the shared humanity then, the universality?

Findley: Yes, it's the universality. It's also that in some instances there are people you get rid of very quickly. They pass in and out of their moment in the book and it hasn't really affected you. They're walk-ons in the true sense.

Interviewers: Like Juliet d'Orsey from *The Wars* who has a 'walk-on' in *Famous Last Words?*

Findley: Did you catch that? Nobody else has caught that. I thought that was good fun. I thought it was really lovely that I had the chance to underscore her existence again. The people who really got to me, some of them were fictional, some of them were real. The Allenbys—I became very attached to them. I adored him. The Allenbys were fiction.

Interviewers: We were sorry when you killed him off.

Findley: Yes, I wanted more of him. Oddly enough, I found myself very caught up in the story of Hess. The whole of the being-driven-mad thing. I wrote it at greater length at one point. I also had T.E. Lawrence in the book.

Interviewers: Why did you take him out?

Findley: There got to be too many people. I was drawn to him as a character. It was the kind of thing you fall upon—an incident. When you're doing your reading, you have this extraordinary spin-off, that there could have been a 'cabal'. You realize that something you made up might really have been. You realize that Bedaux and von Ribbentrop were like this (fingers crossed) in real life. Lawrence, coming toward the end of his last few weeks, one of his last letters was a reply to Margo—a silly lady, Joyce Grenville's aunt—Nancy Astor, he said: "I won't come to Cliveden because I'm not going to get involved in anything again. I'm sick of being involved." She had written to him saying, "You must come. I have some intriguing new people that you should meet and I've an intriguing new thing that I want you to be part of." Then you think, "God, it could have been!" All of it happened there.

Interviewers: All these characters shared a certain sympathy with the Nazi regime and that's all factual, and all of them knew each other...

Findley: And a lot more knew each other than we'd like to think. For a society that now seems so large, it was in fact, a very small group of people. They all knew each other and they all grew up together. They all moved in one relatively tightly-knit circle.

Interviewers: But where do you draw the line between fact and fiction?

Findley: You draw the line when you close the reference books, when you discover the books are getting in the way of the fiction—by which I mean writing fiction.

Interviewers: So they have to live in fiction rather than fact?

Findley: Indeed, they have to, but I never had them anywhere they couldn't actually have been.

Interviewers: About Mauberley, he started off as Pound's fiction and became your fiction. What were some of the problems in that?

Findley: The problems only really came when I had to cut him out. I wanted more of him. I mean it could have been an eight-hundred page novel!

Interviewers: How did you feel about approaching a character like Mauberley?

Findley: In a timorous way, but I had read enough to know that I was not misguided to be doing what I was doing. But I also didn't read so much that I got bound up and constipated with all the academic stuff that could be said about Mauberley.

Interviewers: It raises a lot of critical questions, such as that literature comes out of literature.

Findley: And why shouldn't it? I mean why shouldn't it? It's part of the life of the mind, the civilization. It's no different than writing a novel about the life of Dr. Samuel Johnson. I could write a novel about Dr. Johnson based on his own writings and I can imagine him a highly impassioned man, and a strange man, but only a fool would write a book about Johnson without referring to Boswell. How do we know that Boswell's *Life of Johnson* isn't a work of fiction? But you live by that book—he's one of the great and mighty figures of the English language.

Interviewers: Was Mauberley a hero?

Findley: Yes.

Interviewers: What do you think a hero is?

Findley: Well, I've said this before, so it's going to sound corny, but it seems to me a hero is someone who must do what he must do despite the consequences. Everything else conspires against the doing of that thing. Mauberley is a hero because in writing what he does on the walls he must condemn himself and everything he stood for.

Interviewers: "Including the lies?"

Findley: Including the lies. I can remember being very glad when that line came. At first I thought it was just a clever line and then it became more and more profound. It sets the whole thing up—what is true and what is a lie? Which of these is this?

Interviewers: That also carries over of course into art.

Findley: Indeed.

Interviewers: Is the Grand Elysium Hotel of *Famous Last Words* a type of afterworld for that whole generation?

Findley: Yes. I've never got over that line in Pound of Elysium being the halls of hell. That's what the hotel is like. I had Mauberley take it one step further: "The halls of this hotel are hell because of all the whispering ghosts." But I took out that line. That's why I chose the name Elysium and that image of the gathering-place where everything floats over the abyss.

Interviewers: In your novels, there are characters of great sensitivity and intensity who are essentially non-conformists. Ruth Haddon in *The Butterfly Plague*, Robert Ross in *The Wars* and Mauberley in *Famous Last Words*. Yet they embrace, for a time at least, very regimented constructs, doctrines and ideologies. In Ruth Haddon's case it is the training for the Berlin Olympics; with Robert Ross, it's going into the army; and with Mauberley it is fascism. What are we to make of this? Are you saying that what is tragic about them is that for a time they give in and concede defeat in the battle to preserve their identities, their individualities?

Findley: I think so. I feel very offended by people who write from a point of view saying: "None of this has anything to do with me," and for instance, utter pacifists who say: "I was never anywhere near that war." This is the fascination of someone like Siegfried Sassoon. He believed the opposite of what he did because he was compelled to do both. This is what makes human beings human and therein lies the great fascination of all the people you've just listed. To me, as a writer, the fascination with Ruth is in the fact that she is someone who wants so desperately to have a child. And that's the goal. The child is just a bag of water (a false pregnancy) but it's the human thing to want that. It's what we all want to achieve. The best people try to achieve the best that is in them. Each of these characters you've mentioned has tried that. In doing that, in having passed through the stage where they appear to give in, like Ruth giving in to Bruno and Robert Ross giving in and going to war, and Mauberley giving in to fascism, that is what makes them human. When they come out of that, they have an utter sense of responsibility to the truth. They can't express that truth until they express what they were in the past. Other characters like the Duke and Duchess of Windsor refuse to do this. The largest statement that you can make about them is that they refuse to grow up and live in the real world. They are totally surrounded· by people who want to protect them from reality. The Duke and Duchess try to change reality and fail. The world doesn't want to be run by kids, babies. The thing that breaks you from your childhood is that moment when you lie in bed at night and realize you are not the centre of the world. Some people never have that moment and somehow that has something to do with fascism. When people come out of the bedroom the next morning they either come out reconciled to the fact that they are not the centre of the world—and that's maturity—or they come out and say: "Goddammit! I'm going to be the centre of the world!" They do everything throughout their adult life to try to ensure this.

Interviewers: And this can eventually involve whole nations doing the same thing?

Findley: Exactly. It seems to me you can discover the centre of things and all the great realities and keep them to yourself and so what. These are the very boring heroes and heroines. The ones who accumulate whatever it is they learn about things, what reality is really about and then say "I must change it for them," those are the more interesting people. Robert Ross saved the horses, not himself.

Interviewers: Do all your characters, in order to realize themselves, go through a purging process?

Findley: Not consciously so, but it turns out to be that way in the end.

Interviewers: They all seem to go through a trial by fire. What is it about violence, and especially violence involving fire, that is pervasive in your novels and your play, *Can You See Me Yet?*

Findley: I don't know. I think people are very violent inside, and maybe it has something to do with being consumed by rage or being thwarted by something and it's either something they can't articulate or can't do anything about. I can't account for the presence of fire in my work and I wouldn't want to know.

Interviewers: Why do you have so many rabbits in your works? Did you have any when you were a child?

Findley: Yes I did, and I'll never forget it. One day I had a very traumatic experience. An older boy came into my garden. I had a rabbit and there was a cardboard box. I don't know why, but the boy had in his hand one of those extendable curtain-rods. He put the rabbit under the box and stuck this thing down through the hole and killed my rabbit. I couldn't stop him. I've never forgotten that. It's irremovable. It sits there.

Interviewers: You suggest in your works that people somehow do endure, that memory endures.

Findley: Absolutely. For instance, Mauberley endures because he remembers. In reading Pound's "Mauberley" I found all sorts of things. I found myself ahead of the poem as I wrote and I'd go back to the poem and discover that something that I thought was in the poem was in the book and then it would leap-frog forward and take me forward. You see what I mean? This is the reason why Mauberley became so real to me. I could think like that man. I could be that person.

Interviewers: What about the world where Mauberley exists? Do you see any parallels with the contemporary world? Do you think we're headed for the same sort of fate, such as a world war?

Findley: I think that Mauberley's world was the step that led us to where we are now. We obviously haven't learned a bloody thing. We've only descended further. We now care less about other persons than we did then. After all, people back then did go and fight in Spain. People don't do that anymore. If they do, it's only ten people. Ten, for instance, might go off to El Salvador and then turn up as bodies on the beach. People don't look with a critical eye at someone like Ronald Reagan and say, "You're crazy."

Interviewers: Isn't Reaganism the kind of nationalistic sentimentality that contains the seeds of fascism?

Findley: Of course it is! This is what is wrong with Reagan in my view. However much he may be perceived as being very strong, and I don't mean this in a facetious way, he's a big baby. In fact, what he seems to be conjuring up is a kind of nineteen-thirties movie vision of what America is about.

Interviewers: Do you associate yourself with any particular school of writing?

Findley: No.

Interviewers: Is this something you've consciously avoided?

Findley: No, not consciously. But I went through stages where I knew I was being influenced by other writers, such as Margaret Laurence and Thornton Wilder. I read Wilder's *The Ides of March* two or three times in the course of writing *Famous Last Words*, because he wrote about a whole contained world, the world around Julius Caesar. It's a marvellous evocation of real people with real power. Caesar isn't just a person in power strutting around, he's someone who sits alone at night in libraries musing: "What is really going on here?" But if you write in this time and are really interested in writing and not just being published, sure you're going to end up having conversations with other writers. It's unavoidable. But every single writer will deny that there's any connection or influence. It's the strength to keep writing that's important. That's what you get from other writers. You've got to be yourself. What value are you if you're not? As a writer, that's what you're trying to do. As people, writers aren't important at all, but as people who write they can be important. What one writer writes can be enormously important for another, in a positive way and a negative way.

Interviewers: Do you now see your first two novels, *The Last of the Crazy People* and *The Butterfly Plague* as preparation for *The Wars* and *Famous Last Words?*

Findley: Yes, and in between the first two and the last two there were two unpublished novels, some plays and television dramas. But you know, I say when I get it right, I'll die. That's what you're trying to do—get it right. I'm sure that's why characters in my novels keep popping up who are echoes of previous characters of mine. You must remember that everything is in retrospect. You don't know what you're doing when you do it. You don't sit down and work it out and say: "If I do this it will lead to that." What you think is: "Oh, this is fascinating. I like this." And then you find yourself in the middle of something.

Interviewers: You can't allow other works to be looking over your shoulder?

Findley: No. But sometimes my agent looks over my shoulder and says as she looks over the pages: "Any rabbits?"

Interviewers: What do you hope people will come away with from your novels?

Findley: A sense of having been somewhere with real people, and a sense that they've been moved to struggle with the same dilemmas that I'm struggling with. I would never want anyone to come into a theatre or open a book without a sense of anticipation and a pleasure and all those things. Everything should be a good read, an exciting time to encounter whatever the thing is. But at the same time you do desperately want to stimulate what, in my opinion, is a dying civilization. We could go on and get better but we're dying on our feet.

Interviewers: What can we do to save it?

Findley: Pay attention. Pay attention to real reality and real reality has as much to do with Lynn Seymour and Stravinsky as it does with streetcars and bumping people off at the corner. They're both reality. Squalor is reality, the horrors that surround us as we live here are reality. But art is also reality. The mind is reality. The imagination is reality. We must return to the fact that we have been given the most extraordinary equipment alive, and we're not doing anything marvellous with it, are we? The marvellous is what you want.

James Reaney
Horses, Buggies and Cadillacs

The north end of London, Ontario is much like the setting for a James Reaney play. The streets are lined with older houses and tall trees overarch the wide roads and green lawns. When we arrived on a hot and muggy May afternoon, Reaney appeared at the screen door, tired and breathless. Though it was a very hot day, he wore his trade-mark wool cardigan and black string tie. As he showed us into the front parlor, he explained that he had three plays on the go and would, later that afternoon, have to drive to Waterloo for a workshop involving one of them.

A garbage can in the corner caught our attention. "Is that a map of the world on the garbage can?" Reaney replied: "Yeah. I think there's a message there for somebody to figure out."

James Reaney was born near Stratford, Ontario in 1926 and was educated at the University of Toronto, where he received his doctorate in English literature. Reaney has twice won the Governor-General's Award for Poetry—for *The Red Heart* (1949) and *A Suit of Nettles* (1958). But he is probably

best known for his plays, especially The Donnelly Trilogy—
Sticks and Stones, St. Nicholas Hotel, and *Handcuffs.*

Reaney currently teaches at the University of Western
Ontario and lives in London with his wife, poet Colleen
Thibaudeau.

Interviewers: Tell us about your recent collaboration with John
Beckwith on the opera *The Shivaree.* How did it start and what
was the idea for it?

Reaney: We had done another opera together in 1959 and
called it *Night Blooming Cereus.* John felt we should do something completely opposite in the way of a comic opera—light,
fast-moving, funny. So that's the kind of libretto I tried to
write. He was very interested in percussion at the time and
still is, and in sound, not necessarily music. So the themes that
crossed my mind had to suit the music. That's why I wrote
about a shivaree, which is drawn from my own experience
and because a shivaree is composed of discordant sounds. I
wrote the libretto in about one year and it was finished by
1961. Unfortunately we never got a patron or a commission
for it. John had to wait for a sabbatical in order to work on it.
That's why it has the appearance of having taken twenty
years to write when it actually took only fifteen months to
finish.

Interviewers: There seems to be a contrast, musically, between
the first act and the second.

Reaney: That's intentional.

Interviewers: Did you intend that with the libretto?

Reaney: Yes. You save and you save and you save and you
have these shivaree people in the background and the other
characters are talking about them. There are little hints in the
music about what is going to happen. The little hired boy
goes out and beats the cream-can. You hold back and then in
Act II you let the audience have it. Some people said that Act
II is better than Act I. On the other hand you can't under-

stand Act II without the build-up you have in Act I. I've seen worse Act Ones in many other things.

Interviewers: Act II seemed to lean more towards Borodin, musically, whereas Act I was twelve-tone.

Reaney: To my mind what makes Act II sound so different is that you are getting all those explosive sounds all the time.

Interviewers: How did your collaboration with Beckwith compare with your collaboration with Marty Gervais or Alfie Kuntz?

Reaney: It was much more complex with John Beckwith. I didn't have very much time to work with Marty Gervais. With Kuntz it just got written. We didn't actually do a lot of thinking about putting on *The Bacchae* with 180 people. I couldn't seem to get a story for Alfie Kuntz. But I really tried. The trick is that a lot of poets just go blindly ahead and write and it is too rich for opera. A libretto is merely a stylized story intended to be sung, not recited. The writing has to be especially lean in order for the music to have anything more to say. For example, Dorothy Livesay's operas with Violet Archer or Barbara Pentland accomplish this. What usually happens in many modern operas is that you never hear the words. I carefully wrote mine with many repetitions and rhymes so there is no excuse for the composer or actor/singer not to be able to get those words out. I think seventy percent of the time in *The Shivaree* the libretto was audible, which is a very high percentage.

Interviewers: Do you remember participating in any shivarees when you were growing up?

Reaney: I never actually participated in any but I heard about them as a kid. I heard a lot of stories.

Interviewers: Such as?

Reaney: (Smiling.) Such as in the opera.

Interviewers: The shivaree is a very particular kind of ritual in the folk tradition. Folk tradition of this kind figures very prominently in your work.

Reaney: Yes. I'm very conscious of it. It is interesting that one of my childhood toys was a part of a shivaree band. That's the stylization principle. What I mean by that is that you take a ritual or folkloric tradition, something that people know about and you make it or remake it on your own terms.

Interviewers: Do you think people's culture is preserved more in rural settings than in urban settings?

Reaney: I was born on a farm near Stratford, you see. I'm hooked on that pastoral tradition. I was born into it just as that world was beginning to collapse. I'm just on the edge of horses and buggies and Cadillacs—Cadillacs on blocks in the front yard. It's got a lot of colour. Many of my works play on small-town, agricultural backgrounds; for instance, *The Whistle*. Being born into that kind of world, you never forget it. It becomes the pattern for everything else. It has remnants in it of things that urban culture forgot about years ago.

Interviewers: Is it because urban culture has become too sophisticated or too assimilated?

Reaney: People in the city listen to radio too much and watch too much TV. They're not close to the animal world anymore or the pastoral world.

Interviewers: Do you think that our technological culture is forcing us further and further away from our mythic traditions?

Reaney: It is obvious that we are being forced away from them. It is happening around here, in London. But we also move back into it now and then with poetry readings and drama workshops.

Interviewers: Do you think rural landscape suggests more possibilities, imaginatively and mythically than the urban landscape?

Reaney: Not necessarily, but open landscape always gives you more of a feeling of spiritual forces whereas the city has cubes and squares and lozenges and things.

Interviewers: But in some ways the city can be a kind of refuge.

Reaney: Yes, the New Jerusalem kind of thing.

Interviewers: Such as the feeling Mrs. Donnelly has when she comes to London to escape her neighbours in *The Donnellys*.

Reaney: She's on the run. She's scared. She's running for her life. I think the vigilantes were quite prepared to kill her in London. These are Chicago Irish, the kind who shot people on the street corners in the Twenties, probably in front of the same church each week. (Laughter.)

Interviewers: We understand you've had your creative writing students do reports on the physical geography of various counties in Ontario. Is physical geography important from a creative standpoint?

Reaney: Yes. The modern world tends to blur the physical geography. For instance, regional government adds another layer of municipal government that is unnecessary, that is bureaucratic, that is alienating. In the old days you knew where you were. You had a boundary. You were in Perth County and you identified with the county and the township. You grew up in that. There was a culture there, no matter how faint, and it was generated by the feeling of those identifiable boundaries. That's why I had my students look at regional geography. They had never thought of that before. I'm convinced there's the same sort of feeling about the municipal wards here in London. The various wards are named after saints. People have forgotten all about that. They know they're in Ward One but that doesn't mean very much. It used to mean a lot more. There is an identity here which I've tried to capture but it is rapidly fading. Everything tends to wash out in the sameness of modern society. There's probably nothing that can be done about that either.

Interviewers: Nevertheless, you have spent time in various cities, particularly Toronto, where you attended the University of Toronto. What kind of shaping influence did the University have on you?

Reaney: Very great. It was good to get away from Stratford and the farm.

Interviewers: Who were your professors there?

Reaney: Priestley, Woodhouse, Macgillivray and Knox— mostly people you don't hear of anymore. I had Claude Bissell for a while when he came back from the army. I was in Classics for a time and had Norman Endicott who I liked very much. Endicott was originally from Lucan. He was from a Methodist family.

Interviewers: And you studied under Northrop Frye?

Reaney: When I was taking my Ph.D. I took Frye's Literary Symbolism course and got the idea for *Alphabet* from his lectures.

Interviewers: *Alphabet* depended heavily on the ideas of iconography.

Reaney: Yes, Narcissus, Dionysus and all the rest of them are there in *Alphabet*. It was intended to be a repository of icons and symbols for writer and reader combined, and for the society around them. Whether it worked that way or not, I don't know. A lot of people didn't understand what *Alphabet* was doing.

Interviewers: Do you think that by putting local birds and insects into your works that they will eventually become local icons?

Reaney: I don't really know about that. However, I was conscious when nobody knew what a killdeer was that there was some work that needed to be done.

Interviewers: But doesn't it also serve to make people more conscious of their surroundings?

Reaney: Yes. These things are present in the landscape if people just look for them—things such as killdeers. But those same people seem to be looking at something else. TV probably.

Interviewers: It seems that no matter where you went with *The Donnellys* in Canada you got a good audience response. Why do you think the story about a southwestern Ontario Irish family of the nineteenth century speaks so poignantly to a modern audience?

Reaney: Well, it is partly the Kelley book which they have all read. There was a big influx of people from Biddulph into the rest of Canada after the Donnelly incident and they carried the story with them. So even though they are not directly involved with the narrative, it seems familiar to them. It is partly also the fact that it was very well-publicized at the time. Everyone in Canada and America knew about it. It was a very famous murder. The name Donnelly meant something the way that Lizzie Borden meant something.

Interviewers: Has the total picture of what happened to the Donnellys been cleared up?

Reaney: No, there are still people working on it. What I try to suggest in the play was that the feud was more about land than it was about the Donnellys' behaviour. The genealogy is still being worked out. It was some more intense personal thing about members of the same family. The Carrolls (Jim Carroll led the vigilantes) were related to the Donnellys. It was a fight about land which is like a lot of Irish fights. The Donnellys certainly played into their enemies' hands by thinking so independently. Curious things still keep cropping up about the Donnellys. You can't get to the bottom of it. Their children don't seem to have been baptized in the local Catholic Church. You can't find them in the Christening Book up at St. Patrick's. There's no record of it at any rate. They don't sound like Catholics. Some people say they had their own mind about everything. There's a lot of people like them in Irish history who simply will not give in to other people around them. This goes back to the fact that their ancestors were local chieftains who just fought and fought and fought and never stopped. At the same time, it is interesting how the vigilantes were very effective in getting a whole community swung over to their side. Well, not all of it, but most of it. There are a lot of unknown things about the Donnellys—for instance, the various things they are accused of having done. They are the kinds of things that you hear about in Northern Ireland today and you know there are *agents provocateurs* on both sides.

Interviewers: The family is very much a dominant motif in your work...

Reaney: Yes, but a writer doesn't see such motifs. That's what a critic sees. The writer just sees what he likes. He's not very conscious about this motif business. It is just his personal experience. I had a very happy childhood. I keep going back to that. It is really where you get your first ways of thinking and writing about things.

Interviewers: Were you involved in putting on plays when you were young?

Reaney: Yes. My mother directed plays. My father was in them. I did a lot of play-acting in the neighbourhood, Christmas concerts and such things.

Interviewers: And that kind of experience stayed with you?

Reaney: Yes. Of course a lot of people forget that the schools are now actively encouraging play-acting. More innovative drama is encouraged.

Interviewers: Do you think this makes drama a more universal experience?

Reaney: Oh, yes indeed.

Interviewers: Is this what attracted you to the Peking Opera and the way its productions are staged? You've written about them in the prefaces to several of your works, citing them as an important influence. You saw them tour in 1961 and you've noted it was a very formative experience for you.

Reaney: The Peking Opera is very stylized and anti-realistic. The big jelling factor in Canada in drama was that one could see that movies were very powerful, very dramatic, and Canadian plays seemed boring because they were just talk.

Interviewers: It seems you were also trying to make plays more accessible and less expensive to produce.

Reaney: Yes. While the Peking Opera itself would be very expensive, imitations of the methods used in staging the opera are inexpensive because you can use a lot of cheap props, and in the Peking Opera the audience is asked to imagine a lot. But oddly enough, I remember a lot of the old Samuel French catalogues for play equipment that my mother had. There was a Chinese play in one of them and the instructions for staging it said that you didn't have to have scenery for this and the stage-hands could be visible, moving things around and handing out the props. I read that in 1934, and it stayed with me for all those years. *Our Town* by Thornton Wilder is a North American example of that kind of play.

Interviewers: What are the benefits of workshop production? You've worked in that way more than a lot of other playwrights.

Reaney: Well, you get the chance to write the thing with the actors. You get a chance to try things out, whereas with the approach that I was brought up with you just wrote it and it was put on.

Interviewers: Between the *Jubilee* magazine version of *Wacousta* and the Press Porcépic edition you seem to have enlarged the play considerably.

Reaney: Yes. You know *Wacousta* is a very difficult novel to adapt. First of all it is difficult to find a complete edition of it. The McClelland and Stewart version only prints about two-thirds of it. There had to be big decisions made, for instance changing one character into a woman, so we could get more women in the play. There was an awful lot of critical work involved. We had a *Wacousta* conference here in London in which we got everybody who had ever worked on it to talk about it. The purpose of the workshops was to get the students around here to read *Wacousta*. It was always a despised book. It still is by many of my colleagues.

Interviewers: You seem very influenced by the gothic novel and gothic fictions.

Reaney: That's right. Rider Haggard was one of my deep loves as a child.

Interviewers: Do you think you absorbed the 'gothic' by osmosis and it has come out in most of your plays?

Reaney: Yes. I think Ontario is like that, particularly southern Ontario. They like that kind of work, or at least they used to. Frye taught *Wacousta* in his Canadian literature course when I was a student at university.

Interviewers: During your college years you wrote a short story, "The Box Social," that caused quite a reaction at the time. It dealt with abortion. Have you written any other stories since then?

Reaney: No, I was so discouraged by the reaction against it that I simply didn't write anymore stories. I got put off.

Interviewers: What did they say about it?

Reaney: It seemed like it was the first story that had ever been written in southern Ontario. It was published in a very popular magazine called *New Liberty*. One of the things that always boggles my mind is that you have this kid at college and he publishes a story in the sort of local *Penthouse* of the day and all across Canada you have angry denunciations of it. A publisher in his right mind would immediately say to the kid, "Why don't you do *The Box Social and Other Stories?* Get ten of them out right now and we'll publish them." But they took the opposite stance—that I shouldn't have written it. I'm glad they didn't pick up on it in a way, because I would have been overexposed too early. But I wouldn't mind writing some short stories now.

Interviewers: How do you compare the roles of playwright and poet?

Reaney: They're the same.

Interviewers: Which came first for you, poetry or drama?

Reaney: Poetry. I wrote my first poem when I was ten or nine. I did write a play when I was in high school, but that was the earliest.

Interviewers: What do you think of your critics?

Reaney: I can't afford to worry about the things in my work that they worry about. I've got other things to do.

Interviewers: Has your drama been a process of taking your poetry and making it visual?

Reaney: Yes. And oral too. You're speaking it aloud. You don't just have a reader, you have an audience.

Interviewers: What is your approach to teaching?

Reaney: One thing that I've noticed about my students is that they want lecture notes. They're terrified if they don't have notes to study from. I find that they've all had high-school teachers who told them never to use the word "I." You have all these fantastic passive constructions and you ask them to write about themselves and their own environment and they're in deep trouble. They don't know what to do. I enjoy that kind of project.

Interviewers: Do you try to instill a particular attitude toward literature?

Reaney: Yes, I suppose I do. I don't want my students to be academic fuddy-duddies.

Interviewers: There's a famous story about you bicycling to Toronto from Stratford to see *Fantasia*.

Reaney: With two friends. All the early Walt Disney was terrifically influential on me. It was experimental, wild, not what you usually saw in movies. We'd heard somewhere there was a longer version playing in Toronto so we just had to see that. We'd already seen it twice in the local cinema.

Interviewers: Did the collage effect of *Fantasia* appeal to you? You've used collage in such plays as *Colours in the Dark*.

Reaney: Oh yes, but unconsciously so.

Interviewers: What are your favorite films?

Reaney: Pinocchio and *Great Expectations.*

Interviewers: Do you try for a conscious cinematic effect in your plays and poems?

Reaney: Yes. I want a constant flow of images being juxtaposed, as in a movie. A lot of people, for instance, said that after seeing *Sticks and Stones*, it was a lot like a movie.

Interviewers: Have you thought of turning it into a movie script?

Reaney: Yes, but it would be very different from the play. You wouldn't be able to say all those things on camera that you can say on stage.

Interviewers: In your play, *The Dismissal*, Allan Stratton played Mackenzie King. Do you think that had any influence on him later writing the play *Rexy* which was based on the life of King?

Reaney: Perhaps. He was going to school here in London and was in many workshop productions of mine from about the time he was fourteen. He's a friend of mine. His first play was published in *Alphabet*. I think we talked about Mackenzie King before I wrote *The Dismissal*. I always wanted to do a play like Yeats' *Drums on the Window*, in which King would meet his grandfather through a medium. But I never got around to doing that. But I wrote part of *The Dismissal* for Allan. I knew he could do it and he was dynamite in it.

Interviewers: Mackenzie King also turns up in *Colours in the Dark.*

Reaney: Well, he's there because he was the Prime Minister when I was a kid. I can remember hearing him speak on the radio. He spoke at Stratford and he was a household name, the way Wilfrid Laurier was or Trudeau is today. People didn't like him very much. But he kept getting elected.

Interviewers: How did he do that?

Reaney: I don't know. Whatever brand of poison he was selling, people seemed to like it. (Laughter.) But he was fascinating and he was very Canadian.

Interviewers: You've lived in many places—Toronto, Victoria, Winnipeg—but you always return to this area. why?

Reaney: Family. It is where I was brought up.

Interviewers: What is special about this area of southwestern Ontario for you?

Reaney: I feel at home here. It would be quite different if I weren't born here and just came here later. I'd probably hate it.

Interviewers: How would you define the ethos here?

Reaney: Oh... "Dumb". That's why it is such fun to live here. No one has been over the ground here. I'm practically the first in every field. It is very inarticulate, but it is beginning to change. Alice Munro has changed it a lot.

Interviewers: In 1957 you wrote about the Canadian poet's dilemma. Does the Canadian poet of today face the same dilemma?

Reaney: I suppose he or she does. There are a lot more poets writing today. I don't think you can change Canada that much. Canada is a rather strange out-of-the-way place. But it is just as well it never changes. It is a very happy place to live. I was down in New York on Long Island about a month ago to see a production of *Colours in the Dark*. Gee, when you really see what the outer world is like, it is majestic but frightening. Very competitive. It is much more relaxed up here.

Interviewers: But yet, here, there is an underlying strain of suppressed violence, of darkness in the Canadian psyche, and that strain is evident in many of your works such as *Colours in the Dark*, *Listen to the Wind* and of course *The Donnelly Trilogy*.

Reaney: If you are a playwright and interested in that type of story you need that material. On the surface of the Canadian society you don't see much of that, whereas in New York you see that right there on the streets. Up here it is safe to write about violence because we're not engulfed by it. In New York if you write about violence you are seen to be encouraging it because the society is so violent right on the surface. I don't like Canadian identity questions. The identity is there and we should just relax about it. In Canada, you're dealing with the descendants of people who said no to the spirit of revolution, so they are a bit fuddy-duddy, but interesting, latently violent and exciting, nonetheless.

Dorothy Livesay
Unabashed Romantic

Just as an unexpected January thaw occurred, Dorothy Live-say arrived at the University of Toronto to take up the position of Writer-in-Residence. Evening after evening, both new and established writers gathered in her small room at Massey College for hours of talk, wine and readings. She was warmly greeted by both students and staff and proved to be one of the most active Writers-in-Residence in the University's history. Livesay's return to the University of Toronto, where she had been a student almost sixty years before, became, as she termed it, a "second spring."

Born in 1909 in Winnipeg, Livesay has won two Governor-General's Awards for Poetry for *Day and Night* (1944) and *Poems for People* (1947). As well as being a writer, she has been a social worker, a political activist and a teacher.

Interviewers: Your new book, *The Phases of Love*, deals with the three ages of womanhood...

Livesay: I actually think there are seven. We can't have men having more than us.

Interviewers: What has drawn you to write so much about the subject of love?

Livesay: Well, I'm a Libra, you know, and they say Libras are always falling in love. Perhaps sometimes it has been infatuation. It has been a very strong emotion for me. I don't go to the extent of Katherine Anne Porter who lived to be ninety and had lovers right up to the end. Some people are simply more inclined toward the sexual side of life. My mother was really not at all interested in sex, but I always have been.

Interviewers: Relationships have provided a certain strong energy for you.

Livesay: Yes. they weren't the only sources of energy for me, of course. The natural world has also aroused my emotions. Some of my early poems deal with the Ontario countryside, for example. Yesterday, at a reading, someone came up to me afterwards and remarked that my landscape was more about people than about nature. I've been thinking about that a great deal. I started very early in this direction with my poems about my grandmother—"Green Rain", for example. There were other poems in that first collection, poems about old women, one about an old man and about children.

Interviewers: You don't agree with the statement, then, that when you put a human figure in a landscape you are being influenced by a conservative aesthetic?

Livesay: That is only because we have seen the dehumanization of art in the past century. I do think, however, that Canadian painting has suffered from dealing too much with landscape. So many of the great artists in Europe, you'll find, related the human figure to the landscape. It is a nihilistic, dead-end approach to remove not only the human figure from the landscape, but to move painting into abstract forms. On the other hand, in literature you can't really become abstract because words are so concrete. I'm always observing people. You can see this again in the many short stories I wrote in my teens and twenties. They didn't get published because there were no outlets for the short story in Canada at that time. I think I was just born with this interest in people and how they react in certain situations. You see this in my work.

Interviewers: You said in *The Phases of Love* that it was the poet's task to bring wonder back to the world.

Livesay: I first said that when I was very young, you know.

Interviewers: Do you still think that?

Livesay: I think the poet can have an influence on the course of history. The greatest thing you can defend is the right of human life on this planet. Whitman had a great influence on me when I was young in that he believed in people and the power of people. I've read a lot of poems lately where people, especially young people, have lost faith in humanity and human creativity. This attitude does not help either the writer or the reader; it is like drying up fresh skin.

Interviewers: In *Right Hand Left Hand,* you put the beginning of your political-social awareness as a writer as coinciding with your first great love affair. There is an intertwining in your writing of the romantic and the political. In that intertwining did one element sometimes displace the other? Was there a tension between the romantic and the political aspects of your awareness?

Livesay: The political poems always seemed to be written after a whole series of lyrical love poems. The political poems moved outwards from the personal relationship, but I kept having haunting memories of that first love affair. It is a very difficult thing for a middle-class writer to be able to bring the political facts of life into focus with the personal. In Canada, we've had no working-class poets of any great note. There was of course, Joe Wallace who was a very warm-hearted and loyal member of the labour struggle in this country. His poetry, however, has remained very conservative in its form and almost Victorian in its language because he had not solved the problem of creating a new language out of the new struggle. In Russia it happened, of course. People like Maya-kovsky completely revolutionized the language to suit the struggle. This was not a problem I could solve either. I still used middle-class language because that was what was available to me.

Interviewers: Would you consider someone like Al Purdy a working-class poet?

Livesay: I think he comes close to that in that he had to work at all kinds of jobs to earn his living. And that's another thing you see. The women poets in this country, except now, with someone like Erin Mouré who works on a CNR train, have not worked in the working-class jobs at all. There are, of course, a few working-class women poets. I mentioned Mouré, but there is Gwen Hauser and that girl who committed suicide, Sharon Stevenson. Stevenson began by writing love poems and lyrical poems, which seems to be a natural thing for women. But she was confronted with her deep belief in Marxism and the need for change and perhaps it was that conflict in the long run which made her give up and commit suicide. This problem has not been resolved in Canada. There's a kind of women's poetry developing which is certainly different from the way women used to write. It does not promote the Marxist answer of putting social poetry into the forefront. Instead, it is a social poetry based on casting away all the ideas of patriarchy. So it is getting to be much more widely read. I'm not sufficiently versed in Marxist theory, however, to know whether this is increasing the conflict between feminism and Marxism or whether it will eventually provide a solution. The Marxists say we must change society and that then a lot of women will change. I have turned away from the political struggle to think of the individual struggle. All my later poetry is mostly dealing with relationships.

Interviewers: Can you make a political metaphor out of the individual human relationship?

Livesay: You mean that women will only be free when society is free? Well, I would go into it from this angle: war will only be stopped if women have much greater power than they have now. I suppose more than anything, it has been the sruggle to stop war which has fired me for the past several decades.

Interviewers: Preceding the Second World War you were a member of a pacifist movement...

Livesay: Oh, yes. The League Against War and Fascism, which at one point in the mid-Thirties became the League for Peace and Democracy.

Interviewers: In *Right Hand Left Hand* you did not attempt to impose any hind-sight consistency on the political views which you held at various times...

Livesay: Throughout the book I didn't try to interpret much. I did interpret in a couple of places and now I regret that I published certain paragraphs saying I was a dupe of other ideologies. It wasn't really true. I joined the Left because they were the only group in Canada that were fighting to help the unemployed. It was a genuine battle and no other party except the Communist party was into that. It was a chance to belong to a movement that was really doing something.

Interviewers: Did your political involvement distract you from writing?

Livesay: What I did not do was write the kind of poems I'd been writing. What I turned to was the Brechtian kind of poetry, what they call 'agit-prop'. In that style, I also wrote some plays such as *The Times Were Different*, which is a play about racial hatred. That was also a very strong element in my childhood, the matter of racial tensions. You can see this in the book *A Winnipeg Childhood*. It disturbed me as a child to hear my mother's friends shouted at with words like 'Jew-boy' or 'yid'. We were always very warmly connected with the immigrant girls from Russia and Poland. These were the daughters of families who had sent them from the farms to the city to be mothers' helpers. It was those women who had such warm affection for family life and for children. They gave me more than my own family, than my own mother gave me.

Interviewers: How did you become interested in social work?

Livesay: It was simply seeing what could be done. I didn't feel I knew enough about how the other half lived. But that wasn't the sole reason for going into social work. It was simply that there were no jobs available at the time. I was trained at the Sorbonne and I thought that I would be teaching languages. But in universities there were no jobs, just as today; whereas there were plenty of openings in social work.

Interviewers: About the political views that you held at the time—was there a certain personal cost involved for holding them?

Livesay: There was the battle with my parents. My father thought that if I didn't go in for languages, I should go in for diplomacy. He thought I should go to Switzerland and become part of the international diplomatic corps because I was a journalist and interested in politics. But he didn't realize what sort of politics I had. Instead I went into social work. I worked with families in Montreal, trying to save them from eviction. There was no possibility of doing case-work with families who were up against it. They couldn't even get electricity or coal or food vouchers. The need was so immediate. I resented the fact that people had to live like that. So, I started going out on the picket lines at dawn, handing out leaflets. It was all part and parcel of seeing what society had done to people, and a belief that through the political activity I was engaged in, there was a way out for them.

Interviewers: Did you feel that you had to reconcile your literary pursuits with your political activity?

Livesay: I had to try and see whether the poems could be lyrical and still have the elements of good poems. At the same time I felt that they should carry some sort of political message. That was a real struggle. I had to move from the pure agit-prop thing which we've seen the Chinese use under Mao Tse-tung, literature as a weapon. That was the attitude we had also when I was writing. I had to move from that to something which was a combination of personal voyage and political analysis. That was very difficult. But I think I achieved it in "Day and Night". I had models. I had Day Lewis and Auden and Spender; they were all doing this. Writers in Canada, the U.S. and England were all political activists and the climax came during the struggle for Spain. We all joined against war, against fascism. We were for freedom, a higher culture and for art being a part of people's lives. All that seemed to be crystallized in the struggles of the Spanish people against Franco.

Interviewers: There must have been a severe sense of disappointment when the Fascists won.

Livesay: There was. It was terrible. England and France refused to blockade Spain and so the Fascists brought their arms in and their tanks. Also the infighting among the forces of the left—the anarchists, Trotskyites and Communists— became very confusing for me. The poems such as "Catalonia" come from that period. There are some sombre poems about the defeat of the people. When World War Two came, the whole scene changed completely for me. By the time war broke out, I was married and had a child.

Interviewers: In the Thirties in New Jersey, you were a social worker and worked with blacks there and later for UNESCO in what is now Zambia. What significant differences did you notice between the two black cultures?

Livesay: The major difference was that whereas in the U.S. the blacks were very oppressed, segregated and despairing, the black Rhodesians were involved in struggling for their own independence and "one man, one vote" was the popular cry. It was a chance for me to identify with a revolution which seemed certain to succeed.

Interviewers: You wanted to be on the winning side for once.

Livesay: I sure did! I had to leave a year before they got their independence because my tour of duty was over. But in 1963 I was in Kenya the day independence was declared there, and that was very exciting. It was the wildest scene of happiness you can imagine. Everything I failed to see happen in Canada happened in Africa. Of course, they are having a very tough time in Africa right now because of the world economic situation. It affects them very greatly. But I have to believe that men such as the ones I taught during the early Sixties—I was training them to be secondary school teachers—will make a very big difference in the long term.

Interviewers: What did you become involved with when you returned to Canada?

Livesay: One of the first things I noticed was Earle Birney's activities out in Vancouver. There were day and night sessions of poetry with the Black Mountain poets. There were, for instance, sessions with Charles Olson on the theory of poetry and readings by Robert Duncan. I felt very cut off because nothing I had written had any connection with that movement, and I wasn't about to change and write the way they were. But I did study and listen to it. I hadn't written any poetry in several months, but I began looking at my diaries— the ones I'd kept in Zambia—and from those notes in the diaries I wrote a series of poems. It was not in the style of Olson or Creeley or any of those people. In fact, it was much more direct and dramatic. It was a new style for me.

Interviewers: Did your experiences in Rhodesia (Zambia) have something to do with that?

Livesay: Yes. My relationships with people there were much more open and free. According to the British teachers there, of course, it was shocking the way I went around with blacks. But the blacks were so full of vitality, and so eager to learn, that working with them was a great experience! So, when I came back I was able to write in this much more direct and free style. Yet I was shy about letting anyone see that writing because I wasn't sure of it. Finally, one afternoon Anne Marriott came over to our garden and we had tea and I got up the courage to read her the first draft of "The Colour of God's Face"—there were four drafts actually. The first draft, titled "Zambia", was published in Montreal by a magazine called *Cyclic*. Anne said she thought that it was very interesting and responded to the feeling in it. Eventually "The Colour of God's Face" was published in a pamphlet to raise money for the Unitarian Children's Fund.

Interviewers: We understand that you had some involvement in the Vancouver writers' circle that included Ethel Wilson and Malcolm Lowry.

Livesay: This goes back to the 1940's. The Lowrys were too idiosyncratic to be part of the group. They came to our house several times, but they were beyond needing a writer's group. All this was going on during the War. The greatest people I knew from that period were Lowry and Ethel Wilson. Wilson was a remarkable writer, still not sufficiently recognized.

Interviewers: What about your involvement with Very Stone House and Seymour Mayne?

Livesay: That was after my return from Africa in the mid-Sixties. We published the *Collected Poems of Red Lane*. Red Lane was a myth. He existed, but he was a myth. Of the three Lane brothers, Red was the one who was best-known during the Sixties. He had some terrific poems, mostly against war. I think I helped in the selection of his poems. This was after he died so suddenly of a cerebral haemhorrage. Seymour Mayne and bill bissett instructed me to see if Louis Dudek would publish the book in Montreal with his Delta Press. Louis agreed to publish the poems, but bill bissett did some drawings for it and we thought the two elements were a complete balance to one another. Dudek wouldn't hear of including the drawings in the book. This infuriated bill bissett. We were all set to go to press when Dudek made his decision. So, for

ages, nothing happened to the poems. Then, finally, Very
Stone House got going.

Interviewers: In what ways was Red Lane so different from
other poets? In what ways was he a myth?

Livesay: For one thing, he was a red. He would come down
from the interior of B.C., hitch-hiking. He'd come down to
the meetings and readings in the coffee houses of Vancouver
and start reading some of his own work. Milton Acorn was
there then and he and Red caught everyone's attention.
Milton, Red and I gave a reading in the Spartacus bookstore
together and also in a bowling alley . . . no, no, not a bowling
alley . . . what do they call it . . . a place where they have long
poles and push a ball around . . .

Interviewers: You mean a pool hall?

Livesay: Yes! (Laughter.) A pool hall. You had to speak above
the clacking balls. I still have a tape of Red Lane reading at
that event. From then on, the Vancouver scene just blos-
somed. It was no longer just a polite professional intellectual
group as it had been in the Forties. Then, later, Pat Lowther
came along. She of all Canadian poets hit a synthesis of the
personal and political in her poems about Allende and Neruda. I don't find that same kind of synthesis present in a lot of
young writers today, that sense of commitment and dedica-
tion to liberation.

Interviewers: Speaking of liberation, we were both curious
about that photograph of you and your friends which appears
in *Right Hand Left Hand*. What were the circumstances surrounding that?

Livesay: You are talking about the topless picture?

Interviewers: Yes.

Livesay: There were no circumstances. The editor David
Godfrey of Press Porcépic said that we should use as many
photographs as possible. I told him I had tons of them in an
old trunk, so someone from his press went through all these

things and said, "Oh, look at this! Can we have this?" One of the girls in the photograph is a writer named Jean Johnston and her husband is an amateur photographer. He took the picture. Her husband still had the negative and we asked him to enlarge it.

Interviewers: Why were you sitting there near-naked?

Livesay: We were always having sun-bathing parties at our woods near Clarkson or we'd go to an island in Muskoka and pick blueberries with nothing on. Many young women were doing this. All the things that students are doing today we did back then! We were proud of it. On campus, at the University of Toronto, there was a group of lesbians. There was a group of health-fad people and a group of naturists. Neither Jean nor I thought anything of the photo, but the third person in the shot, the beautiful one, who just happened to be my cousin from England, was quite upset when her husband saw that picture. She was furious at me for allowing it to be put in the book. I just thought that it would never bother anyone today. It is more of a curiosity piece now. You know, I had a weird letter from a nature magazine in the U.S. begging me to let them use this picture. A friend had written them asking them to ask me to write the story about how we were naturists in the Thirties. They sent me a copy of this magazine. It was almost porn! One of those 'sun' magazines. Volleyball! (Laughter.)

Interviewers: You haven't written many poems dedicated to specific people...

Livesay: I try to write for all people. I guess that's the reason why I haven't dedicated very many of my poems to fellow poets or anyone else. There was, of course, my book *Poems for People*. Milton Acorn came along and with my permission used the title in his *More Poems for People*. I was very pleased by that.

Interviewers: Several of your poems have been anthologized quite a bit, such as "Green Rain", and "Bartok and the

Geranium." What sets those poems apart from your other works? Have you been surprised by their choices over the years?

Livesay: Yes. Look at the stupid poems of mine that Margaret Atwood included in *The New Oxford Book of Canadian Verse*. There's no significance to those poems. I mean, they are not bad but they don't lead anywhere really. Whereas the Lecker and David anthology has used some really meaningful poems of mine. They used "Day and Night", for instance. It is stupid of anthologists not to read all of my work in order to find the most interesting and relevant poems.

Interviewers: What do you think is your most popular poem right now?

Livesay: Without question, "The Three Emilys" is the most requested now because of the feminist audiences. That one has not been anthologized yet.

Interviewers: You've often been associated with feminist causes and feminist writing but at the same time various critics have said that you are an "unabashed romantic"...

Livesay: That's someone else's definition.

Interviewers: OK then. What is your definition of a romantic?

Livesay: For me a romantic is someone who is spurred on by a positive view of humanity, who believes in hope rather than despair and who believes in the freedom of the individual above all things. It is to be someone who has not rejected the possibilities of a Utopian society.

Raymond Souster
The Quiet Chronicler

Raymond Souster insisted that he not be interviewed at his home in west Toronto. Instead he met us at a house in the north end of the city. Before the interview began we asked him where he would be most comfortable for a photo session. "Is there a baseball diamond around here?" he asked. As we walked to the diamond, he explained that he liked to keep the various areas of his life separate from one another. Although he has worked as a bank employee in the financial heart of Toronto for over forty years, Souster has still managed to keep up a prolific literary output which includes *The Colour of the Times* for which he won the 1964 Governor-General's Award for Poetry.

The author of over thirty books of poetry and editor of several anthologies, Raymond Souster was born in Toronto in 1921 and has lived most of his life in his native city. A quiet and reflective man, Souster's poetry demonstrates that the simple human acts of day-to-day living are as important as the earth-shattering events of history. His works display an exacting eye for detail, for freezing an instant in time which catches both the subject and the reader completely off guard.

Interviewers: You've been very consistent in terms of your style right from the Forties up to the present. Have you ever been tempted, for instance during the Sixties when a lot more experimental poetry was appearing everywhere, to alter your way of writing?

Souster: Well, I feel, that I have changed my style quite a lot and written in quite a wide variety of forms. But what you say is probably true as far as the critics are concerned. My subject matter perhaps hasn't changed that much, but the form has changed. Maybe I'm more aware of this than the critics are. They probably haven't studied it closely enough. I've been influenced by so many different poets that I feel there is quite a variety in my work. I haven't been influenced by Canadian writers. Mostly they've been American, British, European or South American. This was because when I was first starting to write seriously, there were no apparent major Canadian poets, or at least I was unaware of any. I imitated Archibald Lampman in the beginning, but in Canada there weren't any available models for what I wanted to do. For instance, I couldn't imitate someone like E.J. Pratt and I can't think of anyone else who was readily available for me during the Forties. I had to turn to British poets at first. People like Stephen Spender. Then I discovered the Americans of the Thirties, such as Kenneth Fearing who was a poet of whom I thought very highly at that time. I still like some of his poems but he's been largely forgotten. With someone like Philip Larkin or Thomas Hardy, I admired the content rather than the form. It was the tight metrical structures.

Interviewers: Was it the sadness in Larkin?

Souster: No it was the honesty in Larkin. It was the story-telling quality in Hardy—the dramatic monologues of both.

Interviewers: Do you identify with the urban quality of Larkin's poetry?

Souster: Yes, I can identify with him on that. I understand that Larkin is a great jazz collector so I identify with him in that way too. Charles Olson was an influence as well. From Olson I got the idea of place. The Olson influence isn't the Black Mountain connection. I like the way he wrote about his city, Gloucester, and it made me think I could do the same in terms of Toronto.

Interviewers: Yes, but you are more readable and accessible than Olson.

Souster: That's true, and that's where the critics have tied me in with William Carlos Williams. Williams was important to an extent, but I think his real importance to me was that he served as an example of a very busy professional man who managed to write while keeping up with his job. I identify with that. I write on weekends and in spare moments.

Interviewers: Working in a bank must be a very tiring job. It can take over can't it?

Souster: Right, because it is routine. I suppose all jobs are tiring, but at the bank I work under quite a bit of tension. The deadlines are always there throughout the day. We're always pushing ourselves.

Interviewers: During the Fifties and Sixties you played a leading role in Contact Press, which published the early works of poets such as Atwood and Cohen. What was your role in Contact? How was it founded and why did it end?

Souster: It was begun because there were very few outlets for poetry in the Fifties. Right after the war, very few books of poetry were published. In fact, there were only two or three publishing houses that published poets at all. The poems that Irving Layton, Louis Dudek and myself were writing at the time weren't all that fashionable with the general readership of the period. That, of course, made it even more difficult to get published. We had been published by Ryerson Press in the Forties but by the Fifties it was almost impossible to get published. The idea of a poets' cooperative was dreamed up. Louis carried most of the financial burden. I didn't have much money at the time and I'm sure Irving didn't either.

Louis should get the chief credit for keeping Contact going over that first eight or ten years. Then, when Peter Miller in Toronto came into the picture, he was prepared to put up money so we could bring out two or three books a year, and by that time I think Louis had had enough, so the thing shifted to Toronto. Louis, Peter and I became editors and the three of us decided what books would be published.

Interviewers: We understand that you met Dudek and Layton at the same time that you met John Sutherland. What were the circumstances?

Souster: It was during the War. A chap called Bill Goldberg arrived at the RCAF station where I was in Sydney, Nova Scotia, and Irving was his uncle. Irving had told him to look me up. So Bill and I became fast friends. When I got my next leave I stopped off in Montreal, met Irving, John and Louis, and sort of loosely associated with *First Statement* magazine— to the extent that I had a few poems published in it. But I was generally off on the East coast and so didn't get involved in the battle between the magazine *Preview* and *First Statement.* Unfortunately, no one has really documented that time. I'm hoping Louis will. I know he is writing his autobiography.

Interviewers: Did you feel isolated being on the East coast or in England or Toronto when all the literary action seemed to be in Montreal?

Souster: Perhaps I was better off being isolated and writing from that isolation. I tended to get a lot more work done than I would have had I been in Montreal.

Interviewers: You avoided getting caught up in the politics?

Souster: That's right. That's the danger of all these groups. The politics takes over and you produce less work. I'm a loner and I think I prefer it that way.

Interviewers: Childhood is a very important time for writers. What stands out in yours?

Souster: Nothing that seems very important right now. I went to the University of Toronto Schools for five years and I discovered poetry there.

Interviewers: Is that when you first started writing?

Souster: Yes. It was the biggest thing that happened in my teens. Other than that my life was studies and playing baseball. I was crazy about baseball—not that I had any illusions about becoming a professional but I really loved the sport. My Dad was a baseball fan and he encouraged me.

Interviewers: What was it that drew you to poetry?

Souster: I guess it was reading it and the fact that I was a solitary. I had friends when I was playing baseball but I didn't have friends in the usual sense, and I don't today. I'm just not a person who makes friendships. I've had a lot of acquaintances and I still do. I started work when I was eighteen and went in the service when I was twenty. When you're in the service you're really on your own. You have a lot of buddies, but you move around a lot. I was in one place for two years and another place for a year. There's no feeling of permanence in a life like that and I suppose that's why a lot of people like it.

Interviewers: You've written a lot about World War II. Do you remember where you were and what you were doing when war was declared?

Souster: I remember the day Hitler invaded Poland because it was the day I started work in the bank. I started at eight o'clock in the morning and at midnight I was still in the bank because all the foreign exchange had been taken over by the government. Nobody knew what was going on so everybody was told just to stay at the office.

Interviewers: What stood out for you during your wartime service?

Souster: Well, you see I was stationed on the East coast and so was isolated from the major theatres of war. I was on a home-watch station and our airplanes went out to escort the convoys. In the summer of '42, half our squadron went up the St. Lawrence looking for U-boats, and the boats that brought the ore from Belle Isle to Sydney were torpedoed and for three weeks the steel plants in Sydney had to shut down. But really it was just day-to-day routine work. We didn't really feel we were in a war at all. Anything I've written about the war since has been largely an effort to find out what happened. Many of the best books about the war are just coming out now because the government archives have just been opened up.

Interviewers: Your "Pictures of a Long Lost World" series seems to be an attempt to find out what happened, not only in World War II but in other eras of history as well.

Souster: Yes. I have five or six more poems for that series, poems about my father in World War I. These are things he's just been telling me in the last month.

Interviewers: You came back to Toronto after the War. How has Toronto changed for you since then?

Souster: Well, Toronto was a very sleepy, Anglo-Saxon city. It was the same when I came back from the war. I was born in the west-end and have lived all my life in the west-end and I'm still there but I don't know the rest of the city very well. The only part I can say I really know is my own little district, the Runnymede area. I'm not a very adventuresome person. I've just tried to zero in on what I do know—tried to make that my little world, I suppose.

Interviewers: And that little world seems to contain a nature-versus-city dichotomy.

Souster: Perhaps the nature part of it is the yearning for the old unspoiled Toronto and the other is the reality of the city, which I don't particularly like. I'm sympathetic to the people who have to exist in it, but I'm not particularly in love with it.

Interviewers: Baseball diamonds are like small oases in the urban landscape for you, and you've written a lot about baseball.

Souster: Yes, I really liked the old Maple Leaf Stadium. There was always a good crowd there, especially in the playoff games. In those days the International League in which the Toronto Maple Leafs played was the top farm league for the majors, so the baseball was of a very high calibre.

Interviewers: Did you ever attend any of the games at Centre Island?

Souster: No, that was before my time. That team moved over to the mainland in 1926 and I was about five then. But my Dad used to play there. The bank had a league at Hanlan's Point. He used to go over to all the games, as he was a teller at the bank. He remembers seeing Ty Cobb play. My Dad was the one who really got me going on baseball and as soon as I could throw a baseball I was out there with him.

Interviewers: Baseball seems to be more than just a game for you.

Souster: Yes. It's hard to explain it. When I see someone make a nice double play, well that's ballet. There's a grace in the movement of the players that you don't see too much in hockey any more. Baseball, which doesn't depend on brute strength or body contact, allows more room for other feelings. It's a nineteenth-century game that is still played practically the same way.

Interviewers: Is the great play in baseball something like the instants of perception you try to underline in your poems?

Souster: Yes. If I was a photographer, I'd be trying to catch it in a picture. The little moments—moments of truth I guess you'd call them—occur in the most unlikely places and that's what I try to capture.

Interviewers: You've been active on the Toronto poetry scene for some forty years. What do you think of that scene today?

Souster: I don't really think there is a scene. I don't think there's any Toronto school of poetry, because there are so many different kinds of poetry being written here. I don't think there's anything that unifies them.

Interviewers: But you did try to strive for some sort of unity when you founded the League of Canadian Poets.

Souster: Everyone felt strongly at the time that it should exist. Expo '67 came along and there were plans for a world poetry conference, but there was no body that the government could turn to for guidance, except the Canadian Authors' Association, which really didn't represent Canadian poets. We felt that we needed something better to be the voice of Canadian poetry. Most poets in Canada are very suspicious of organizations. I remember when we had our first meetings down east at Ralph Gustafson's place. There was a lot of skepticism and I don't think anyone was prepared to do much work on it. It was just a wonder it was ever started but I felt strongly about it, and I persuaded a few other people and it actually did get off the ground. I was chairman for two terms.

Interviewers: Who was at the founding meetings?

Souster: Louis Dudek, Frank Scott. There's even been a controversy about who was at these meetings. Of course Ralph Gustafson and Doug Jones who lived next door were there. Michael Gnarowski was there for one meeting. You can't expect too much from a league or an organization, but it has served a useful purpose.

Interviewers: Just after the war you wrote some prose fiction under the pseudonym 'Raymond Holmes'.

Souster: Yes, I did that simply because I wanted to keep my poetry sèparate from my prose, and I didn't have very much confidence in my prose writing. The pseudonym was a wise decision and I've since published another novel under the pseudonym John Holmes, *On Target*, an air-force book. I felt it wasn't that great either, so I just felt better having it under another name. Holmes is my middle name.

Interviewers: You once wrote that you write out of either desire or guilt.

Souster: Well, those are two pretty standard human emotions. I guess everyone has got to carry around a certain burden of guilt when there are people unemployed or starving or living miserable lives. I certainly feel it. What's even worse is that there is so little you can do about it. I think in a lot of my poems I've tried to make people more aware of what's happening just by focusing on the derelicts and so on, people you probably wouldn't give a second glance at. Maybe through reading my poetry, people become more aware of them and don't treat them as just curiosities. I don't think derelicts are people who are looking for pity from poets or anyone else. Many of them are probably ex-business executives who have got the way they are through alcoholism. They are bewildered people and they have to go through this and they either pull themselves out or go under. Except for circumstances, we could be there. I think it is important that we not forget these people.

Interviewers: What is your view of the role of the poet in society?

Souster: Well, the poet's role in, say a Communist society, is much more important because he is the actual voice of his people; he has to speak out against the regime. In Canada, the writer is at the lower end of the social spectrum, and the poet is at the bottom of that heap. I write a lot of low-key poetry. I don't give readings any more because for me they were empty experiences. I understand people that have to, but I'm just not that type of public figure. Writing in the Western world isn't a respectable profession.

Interviewers: Do you consider yourself more of a quiet chronicler then?

Souster: Yes, that's it. I write very low-key poetry and that suits me. I don't want to be known to my fellow workers as a poet. I don't go in for grandstanding because, as I said, I'm more interested in those little moments of truth that occur in the unlikely places, the private places.

Gwendolyn MacEwen
The Magic of Language

We stood anxiously on the porch of the white stucco town-house in Toronto's Annex district, as storm clouds gathered above the late spring day. Up the street a familiar figure rounded the corner on a bicycle.

MacEwen: Sorry I'm late. Hope you haven't been waiting long. C'mon in.

She showed us into the front room of the downstairs flat, where a bay window full of hanging plants, a large Arabian brass jug by the fireplace and an Oriental carpet gave the room a slightly exotic quality. Then, like a Gaelic storyteller, MacEwen took up a seat on the hearth where she sat cradling her grey and white cat.

Gwendolyn MacEwen was born in Toronto in 1941 and was educated there and in Winnipeg. She won the Governor-General's Award for Poetry for *The Shadow Maker* (1969).

Interviewers: The epigraph in your most recent book, *The T.E. Lawrence Poems*, suggests that you felt that you were given a mission to write these poems.

MacEwen: First of all, that epigraph is very ambiguous and misleading because a couple of reviewers have picked up on the date 1962 and assumed that ever since 1962 I've been writing these poems, thinking that it is really some very massive work. But, in fact, I wrote them in one winter, the winter of 1981-2. I had been thinking of eventually writing a book of this kind since the early Sixties, since my trip to Israel and even before. I think I put that epigraph there because the idea of the old photographs of Lawrence was very evocative, those old sepia-tone photographs. Also, I did find out after I'd written all these poems that my 86 year-old aunt Maud had known Lawrence when he was in Dorset. She assumed that I had known this, but I did not know of this family connection at all. In fact, her son, my cousin, Larry, was named after Lawrence.

Interviewers: Was there any intended irony in the epigraph in that you saw in Israel a photograph of Lawrence, who was a former leader of the Arab nations.

MacEwen: It is highly ironic, but I didn't mean anything much by it.

Interviewers: In one of your early poems, "One Arab Flute", there are several lines which turn up again in *The T.E. Lawrence Poems*, about someone playing a flute and there being "anarchy between his fingers".

MacEwen: That's right. I'd never made that connection. You've just done it for me. But they're not *exactly* the same lines.

Interviewers: You seem to rely, in drawing your portrait of Lawrence, on primary sources, such as *The Seven Pillars of Wisdom, Revolt in the Desert* and *The Mint*...

MacEwen: Yes, but I did read everything else I could about him, including recent works which try to debunk his legend.

I've also read the ones that try to make a hero of him, and I don't believe either side. But I believe a little bit of all of them. For instance Robert Graves's book, *Lawrence and the Arabs*, is not to be trusted, because Graves got a lot of his information directly from Lawrence. A lot of the time Lawrence was deliberately leading Graves along. I did a kind of comparative research, but ultimately, when in doubt, I relied on Lawrence's own words—knowing, however, that he told a lot of tall tales.

Interviewers: Lawrence also translated *The Odyssey . . .*

MacEwen: Yes. I have a copy of it. It was dreadful work for him. He hated it. But he just kept ploughing away at it.

Interviewers: Aware as you were that Lawrence was a myth-maker, it must have been quite a challenge to develop an honest narrative voice in the poems.

MacEwen: It had to be a voice that was honest in its dishonesty. It had to be accurate in its inaccuracy. I wanted to sound as deliberately ambiguous as Lawrence himself was. In the poem "Tall Tales" I end with "what if the whole show was a lie and it bloody well was—would I still lie to you?" And the answer is yes. That is the kind of tone I wanted to capture.

Interviewers: Lawrence seemed to make some connections between middle-eastern and Mediterranean cultures. This seems to be a feature of your work too. What is it about the Mediterranean world that fascinates you?

MacEwen: I'm drawn to the richness of the mythology and history. I somehow think it is very Canadian to be drawn to these exotic places.

Interviewers: Because Canada isn't exotic?

MacEwen: Because we don't have an ancient history. So, I'm drawn to countries that do. That in itself is very Canadian. It is the opposite of *here*. *There*, there is so much energy crowded into a small space, whereas here it is spread out over great distances. But I am beginning to see Canada as the most exotic land of all.

Interviewers: In *Mermaids and Ikons* you characterize Greeks as people with a fervent involvement with the present day. Is it possible for you to characterize Canadians in the same kind of one-liner fashion?

MacEwen: Canadians are not really living in the present at all. We're always waiting for something to happen or pondering over things. You see, your main concern in Cairo is getting from one side of the street to the other without being killed. You don't have any time at all to ponder over the pyramids. The same holds for Greece. You are thrust into the present. It is impossible just to go there and ponder. You are forced to consider how myth is operating in modern life; myth is present everywhere in everyday life.

Interviewers: It's the anxiety of anticipation then that keeps North Americans going?

MacEwen: Yes. We are not really comfortable in the present in the way that people are in the Mediterranean countries. They seem to possess the present, even though they are surrounded by the past. As I found in Egypt on an earlier trip, it is the tourist who is weighed down by the past and not the inhabitants of the country. So, I was prepared when I encountered the same thing in Greece. There's no passionate interest there in the past or in the future. They, therefore, avoid being swallowed up by either. But one gets so exhausted by the pace of life and language in these countries. Here people speak much more slowly and carefully. It comes as a relief. You come out of a kind of hysteria over there and Canadians, by contrast, seem very sane and quiet.

Interviewers: In the poem, "Reviresco: For Padraic O'Broin", you wrote: "I cast about always for another tongue". Also, in the poem, "Celtic Cross", you touched on your own Scottish past. But you seemed to have moved away from that.

MacEwen: Well, at this point I think I'm coming back to a consideration of my real roots, which are in Scotland and England. I haven't thought about them for many, many years.

Interviewers: How did you go about looking for the other pasts?

MacEwen: When I wanted to explore the Greek and Arab worlds, I decided that one of the best means of access was through learning the languages of the region, so I studied Arabic and even did some translations, and picked up enough colloquial Arabic to survive—but most of this is forgotten, although I can still read and write a little. I am still reasonably fluent in modern Greek, which I have spoken for some years. I find it very exciting to speak in another tongue, to learn a language other than English. It takes me back to the essential magical elements of language itself, the essence of utterance. I'm interested in language as a magical power in itself.

Interviewers: Is Lawrence the bridge then between the past explorations of exotic cultures and your own heritage? He was also someone who tried very much to understand and appreciate other cultures.

MacEwen: Yes, I identified with Lawrence from the very beginning for exactly these reasons. He was a sort of mad, poetic hero, rushing away, seeking his past elsewhere, seeking some kind of ancestral mythical thing. He also wanted to be a poet, but didn't manage to succeed. He wrote a few poems, but they were awful.

Interviewers: What was it that decided you on a career in poetry?

MacEwen: I started writing seriously when I was about fifteen. Most biographical notes have it wrong when they say that my first poem was published in *Canadian Forum* when I was fifteen. I was actually seventeen, but perhaps that was it—the early publication. Perhaps that's what decided me on being a poet. Plus the fact that I was driven to write poetry all the time.

Interviewers: What was driving you?

MacEwen: I don't know, but obviously since I felt driven it seemed to me that this was what I was supposed to be doing.

Interviewers: Was there anyone in your family who urged you to go ahead and write?

MacEwen: My father was very supportive, but no one in my family wrote.

Interviewers: Early in your career you were involved in the magazine *Moment* . . .

MacEwen: Milton Acorn and Al Purdy were involved in it and I helped with a couple of issues. It was a very small mimeographed magazine.

Interviewers: The "Bohemian Embassy" was also part of your early exposure to the poetry scene in Toronto. What do you remember about those days?

MacEwen: Well, I remember that the "Embassy" had poisonous coffee and that it was very dark. It was dark and you sat around trying to play chess. It was really an extension of the coffee-house scene of the late Fifties. It did set a trend in that it was *the* place for poets in Toronto.

Interviewers: Your first two books were *Selah* and *The Drunken Clock.*

MacEwen: Yes, they were privately printed. They were pamphlets or chapbooks, not books.

Interviewers: How did you decide on the name Aleph Press for your private press?

MacEwen: Because it is the first letter of the Hebrew alphabet. I was my own agent and distributor for them. Back then it was the only way to start—to get one or two chapbooks out and get them around.

Interviewers: Contact Press published one of your books just as that press was winding down.

MacEwen: Yes, Raymond Souster and Peter Miller had seen some of my work and thought that it was time for a book from me. I think it was one of the last books they did, *The Rising Fire.*

Interviewers: Your poetry seems to be remarkably apolitical...

MacEwen: I don't think it is possible to be apolitical. I don't think any form of writing can be apolitical. Writing is concerned with human destiny in one way or another and that involves social or political destiny as well as spiritual destiny.

Interviewers: And the mythic element ties the social and spiritual destinies together. So, it is possible to read a poem such as "You cannot do this to me" as a political poem.

MacEwen: Well, sure, I find that the word "political" is just a word to me. I don't think writers should be propagandists or have strictly "political" causes. I think it limits them and art deals also with paradox, with mystery. I think, however, art inevitably is political by being concerned with Man.

Interviewers: In an article in *Canadian Literature*, "MacEwen's Muse", Margaret Atwood stated that you seem to be a poet who is less concerned with turning your life into myth than translating myth into life.

MacEwen: Yes. A really powerful observation. I remember being deeply struck by it. It is deadly accurate.

Interviewers: But what goes into the process of translating myth into life?

MacEwen: Partly by travelling and doing things. I went to Egypt and Israel; I learned Greek and lived among the Greeks. I want to live myth, not read about it. Finally, I'm not really concerned about literature at all but about life, in its broadest sense.

Interviewers: You make an interesting connection between language and myth. The two seem to be closely associated for you. Is there anything in particular which has led to that fusion?

MacEwen: I got there instinctively I think. This gets back to what I was saying before about the magical power of language, of things being revealed and understood through language and only through language.

Interviewers: Turning to your specific poetic influences, you've cited Hart Crane and Dylan Thomas as the most obvious. but in *The Harsh and Lovely Land*, Tom Marshall remarked that you are a female version of Michael Ondaatje or Leonard Cohen. Do you agree with that?

MacEwen: (Laughter.) What would I *look* like then? It is interesting that you said that because Michael Ondaatje is my favorite Canadian poet. Yes, I can see that in terms of their lushness and their romanticism. Hart Crane is an influence because of what he did with language. And Dylan Thomas for the same reason, but less so.

Interviewers: When you write a poem, do you start from a picture, or the sound of the words?

MacEwen: I start from something which is a fusion of the sound and the picture. I usually hear the lines as they go through my mind, so I guess I do hear it before I see it.

Interviewers: You've also written in prose. In the novel *King of Egypt, King of Dreams*, you treat an epic topic, the reign of the pharaoh Akhenaton. There has been a fair amount of controversy about what you were actually trying to do in that book. You seem to be warning about the dangers inherent in any kind of monotheistic system.

MacEwen: I guess I was attempting to show the dangers of a particular kind of mysticism. Akhenaton is a failed mystic. I wanted to show the dangers involved for someone seeing only good and evil as separate forces, unable to see the overall truth as a dialectical experience.

Interviewers: So, for you, organized religion is too absolute?

MacEwen: Yes, I hate organized religion. I hate any religion which says that *goodness* is against *evil*. My idea of the truth is a fusion of opposites. Jan Bartley in her book *Invocations; the prose and poetry of Gwendolyn MacEwen* says it beautifully when she writes about the *conjunctio oppositorum*, the marriage of opposites.

Interviewers: In your book of short stories, *Noman*, the final story seems to be a summation or a pulling together of the other stories. Were you trying to give a certain symmetry to the work?

MacEwen: Yes. I wanted to round it out. They originated as separate stories, but I realized when I put them together that the central figure in all of them really was one man. It all came together in the character of Noman. I'm now working on a book which is a sequel to the Noman story. Noman, of course, is the name Ulysses uses with the Cyclops. It just hit me that Noman could be a central character in a Canadian novel.

Interviewers: Rather than Everyman?

MacEwen: Yes, exactly.

Interviewers: Is it the role of the writer to identify, to describe, the mythic within the realm of the everyday?

MacEwen: I don't know if it is the role of every writer, but it is my role as a writer.

Interviewers: You once said that you write because you cannot convey the exact quality of your dreams and visions. Does a writer then, out of necessity, have to be a perfectionist?

MacEwen: That I don't know. I am. I'm not so much a perfectionist in writing as I am in the trivia of everyday life. I'm a terrible perfectionist.

Eli Mandel
Double Vision

He explained to us that the painters and workmen who were refurbishing his North Toronto home would make it difficult for us to talk inside and he led us into his back garden. The painters had removed the old wooden screen-door and propped it against the overgrowth at the end of the small yard. The door, propped as it was at an odd angle, looked as if it stood by itself and opened into nowhere.

Mandel: Do you know the picture my wife Ann took in *Out of Place* of the door standing by itself in the middle of the prairie? This kind of looks like it doesn't it?

Mandel moved toward his kitchen door which seemed even more awkward and out of place when he pointed it out to us. For a man who is acutely perceptive of the presence and repetition of metaphors in the imaginative cosmos, both in his own work and the work of others, it seemed appropriate that he would want his picture taken standing beside the door.

Poet, critic, teacher and traveller, Eli Mandel was born in Estevan, Saskatchewan in 1922 and attended the University of Saskatchewan until he left to serve in the Army Medical Corps during the Second World War. After the War he resumed his studies and earned a doctorate in English at the University of Toronto. He has taught at the College Militaire de St. Jean, the University of Alberta and York University. In 1967, he won the Governor-General's Award for Poetry for *An Idiot Joy.*

Interviewers: We understand that you are currently working on a new book entitled *The Family Romance.* What is the significance of that title?

Mandel: The title *The Family Romance* comes from Harold Bloom's *Anxiety of Influence* and refers to the Freudian situation in the family. Bloom is concerned not with the New Critical approach to reading poetry—that is, not a close reading of the poem—but rather with what is called intertextuality. This is the relationship between poems rather than just the poem itself, the influence of one poem upon another and the influence of one poet on another. This has its Freudian relationship in the parallel between father and son. Without going into the details of Bloomian theory, I'm interested in the tradition of poetry in Canada, the relationship of one poet to all the previous poets, and how, as we become most conscious of our past, we handle our past. That seems to me to be one of the major questions poetry is concerned with. *The Family Romance* is in part the story of the poet's relationship with his fathers or the poet's relationship to her mothers and the struggle one has to go through to transcend the family to become one's own voice.

Interviewers: So it's very Oedipal?

Mandel: Yes, very Oedipal. It is particularly intriguing for me because my own relationship with my father and all my fathers is the primary relationship in all of my poetry and in all of my work, and my own life. I think my life began to define itself when I realized that the definition had to be in terms of Oedipal relationships.

Interviewers: Do you have anybody that you consider to be your poetic father?

Mandel: Well, yes. Some people who aren't usually associated with my work now. Kafka, Dostoyevsky, Thomas Mann. The European writers in general seem more important to me now than they once were. Pablo Neruda was a significant figure and then, of course, the moderns in English literature—Yeats, Pound, Auden, Eliot. I suspect it is the moral considerations of the Europeans that attract me. They are less concerned with technical questions than say Auden is. Auden says that any new poem derives from a solution to a technical problem. But I don't think you get that sort of answer to that kind of question from Mann or Kafka. With them, it would be a very singular moral question that would be discussed, such as the nature of evil.

Interviewers: There seems increasingly to be a movement toward more social criticism in your poetry.

Mandel: I wouldn't say increasingly. I'd say that's been my concern all along. For instance, I like to talk about the actual treatment of the Holocaust in literature, for it has become exactly what Adorno predicted it would become—a prettify-ing of the actual event, in a very curious and terrifying way. We begin by talking about the history of the victim of the Holocaust and this is the pathos of suffering and the horror of suffering we are talking about, and we can't stand to look at this kind of thing at all. Gradually, as the years go on, the emphasis changes from the victim to the victimizer, from the Jew to the Nazi. The shift is from the person who suffers to the demonic torturer. The satanic figure has a certain glamour about him. It is this glamour, and I think 'glamour' is the key word, that is dangerous, but which draws us because he is more interesting; the victim is not. As Adorno says: "After Auschwitz, no poetry." Because the moral question was so enormous, we couldn't give it aesthetic value at all. Now we see why.

Interviewers: You try to come to grips with this in your poetry.

Mandel: Yes, it is the problem of evil in the world.

Interviewers: You imply in *Life Sentence* that the elements that created the Nazi state are still with us. The political impulse to control, oppress and torture people is still there.

Mandel: What becomes the dilemma for the serious writer is how to write about these kinds of things.

Interviewers: Without becoming an ideologue?

Mandel: Exactly. If you simply detail the tortures too much, you lose the aesthetic effect. But if you are more concerned with aesthetic effect you lose the significance of the torture itself. That's a dilemma I don't think you can get out of easily.

Interviewers: So that's the difference between an Amnesty International Report and someone who is tortured in one of the jails and who writes a poem about his experiences?

Mandel: Right. Precisely. Precisely that kind of thing. I feel that is quite a dilemma. I'm not sure how you handle it. I felt in *Life Sentence* that the poems were on the edge of toppling into a pornography of violence. Merely recording the violence makes your poem a pornographic poem. You want to avoid that kind of thing. How do you avoid it? You end up by making yourself a victim and then you get caught up in the problem of the banality of evil. You know Leonard Cohen's comment in *Flowers for Hitler:* "I refuse the universal alibi". But, of course, there is no universal alibi. That's the point; he's quite right in refusing it. But even by saying it he brings it into the action of the poem.

Interviewers: Which writers do you think engage in the pornography of violence?

Mandel: Well, Irving Layton. He's toppled over onto the wrong side several times and various other writers in our century. John Berryman, in some of his works, and in certain aspects of Robert Lowell. Certainly in aspects of Ted Hughes and Sylvia Plath, there is this toppling over into pornographic violence of one kind or another.

Interviewers: Does this spring from an over-identification on their part with the victimizer?

Mandel: Plath is awfully interesting in this because she tries to say we're all Jews—I'm a Jew, you're a Jew—but no one ever really believes her. Her cry, which is a very powerful, genuine poetic cry fails because she finally glamorizes the very thing she is trying to tear down, the degenerate glamour of the Nazi era.

Interviewers: In "Images of Prairie Man", you write that the artist moves between the end toward which he is impelled and the beginning where all was foretold. You're given us some indication of what you are impelled toward, but what was foretold for you back in Estevan, Saskatchewan?

Mandel: You see how very much it connects with the thing we begin with. You wonder how much we are foretelling our own future as we conduct these searching questions and answers. You wonder how much the structure of our thought is directed by the place we begin from. For example, why did we begin with talking about *The Family Romance?* That was of interest because that's what I'm working on at the moment. When you ask what was foretold, it seems to me that what was foretold was the fate of an Oedipal child. What was foretold was the fate of a Jewish son who felt he could articulate his destiny. But if you are Oedipus you can't articulate your destiny. It is a doom. He discovers he is lost, and the poetry was not the liberation he thought it was, but the articulation of his fate. This is one of the things Harold Bloom is saying, and I love the way he says it, that we are all belated Romantic poets. We come late, we come after, and because of that we live out a particular kind of destiny. We are involved in a structure of poetic thought which is partly a resistance to our elders, to the literal father and mother and also the poetic father and mother, and consequently there's a pattern: the future is foretold in that. So it goes back to the magazines and books I read. I read *Doc Savage*, which is in the form of romance, which is precisely the romantic quest theme. Of course I was fascinated by that because it was what I wanted to write about. I discovered that the line I was concerned with was the descent quest, which Frye sees as the central question in Canadian writing—the fall into the wilderness of time and space, which is equivalent to the literal environmental fall into Canada. Your geography is equivalent to your metaphors of poetry. When that equivalent became clear to me, then poetry became possible. That's where the future is foretold. I didn't know what these things meant. I just knew that there was power in these images for me. I've only been able to understand this recently.

Interviewers: The Daedalus/Icarus myth seems to have had a lot of power for you.

Mandel: Well yes, it's the fall that is terrifying, particularly when you are a sixty-year old father, engaged in the process of falling yourself.

Interviewers: Does the labyrinth remain an important symbol for you?

Mandel: Yes. It is the wilderness of space and time, which I said was Frye's metaphor for the poetic myth. We're in the situation where we live out our antithetical quest, which is identical with our literal environment in Canada. We can say that the encounter with the wilderness is the Canadian situation. I come from the Prairies and they are a gigantic space. Kroetsch calls it an absence, a void of space and time, a place where nothing is. That is also the labyrinth. Physically and environmentally, place, metaphor and myth, become identical. It took me a long time to understand this. I had always thought they were separate.

Interviewers: So getting back to the question of where your quest began, do you think it started when you left Estevan and joined the Canadian Army Medical Corps?

Mandel: I have a feeling that first there was something that happened in Estevan. It has to do with caves in the valley. If you look at the poems you'll find those images repeated. I don't understand what that's all about. There were caves in the valley, the Souris Valley in Estevan, and we used to as boys go and explore some of these. They weren't big caves. They seemed to me to be symbolic in a deep way which I never understood. I think things began just a little bit before I left Estevan. The caves were symbolically the entrances to, or the exits from, the labyrinth.

Interviewers: Why did you join the Army Medical Corps?

Mandel: There was war. I remember in May of 1943 I was twenty years old and I came to the realization that I had come to the end of the time for not joining the army. I'd gone to school, I'd gone to college, and I thought what am I going to do now? I didn't want to go on in college and so I joined the army. I simply said one night, I have to go. It seemed very important to be part of that. I had had an education in pharmacy for one year at university, and because I'd been an apprentice in a drug store I had some connections with medical training and they put me in the medical corps. It was not a choice. It was just a thing that happened.

Interviewers: William Burroughs has said that his life has been shaped by his two undeveloped careers—medicine and espionage. Do you think your undeveloped career has been an influence on you?

Mandel: Well, medicine has certainly been an undeveloped career with me. I served in the army as a medical storeman and I looked after goods of various kinds—a warehouse man. Bob Kroetsch made a pun on that once about warehouse and whorehouse, but that's not the case. Another undeveloped career was probably in science.

Interviewers: Did your career in the army later influence your decision to teach at a military college?

Mandel: Again, accident plays a tremendous role. I got into the military college because that was the only job available for me at the time that I graduated. I also felt an obligation because I was put through university as a result of my career in the military. I went through on Department of Veteran's Affairs support, right through to my Ph.D. I loved teaching at the Military College. One of my students was Graeme Gibson. It was the only time students ever stood up when I came into a classroom.

Interviewers: Do you miss that?

Mandel: Yes. (Laughter.)

Interviewers: What made you start writing poetry and what were the influences on you, such as particular teachers who encouraged you?

Mandel: It is easy to mythologize this kind of material, and I feel I actually start doing it as the years go by. To the best of my recollection, I began writing very early. My earliest recollection is writing a detective story when I was eleven. I was trying to impress my mother. I began writing poetry in my adolescence, romantic poetry in the style of Keats and Shelley. One reads Keats and Shelley in school and one begins to write like them. I was influenced in my understanding of poetry by a Scotsman, Mr. Fife, who was a very good teacher in my high school. And that's my mythology. That's how I remember it. I was probably also influenced by an uncle of mine, Alex Berner, who played a great role in my sense of what was morally important. I began to publish poetry in college in 1942 before I went into the army. One of those poems was published in the college magazine and widely reprinted across the country. It was a poem about the names of Russian towns. I can still remember some lines, terrible but... you're going to get a genuine scoop here.

When the nights are dark in Russia
Be it Leningrad or Omsk
From the Dneipre to the Tomsk
From something... to...

It played with that idea. The whole poem went along in that kind of rhythm, in quatrains, playing with the concept of names. I wrote rhetorical poetry, romantic poetry at that stage. That's juvenilia. And one doesn't want that kind of thing found again. After that I went into the army and an absolute transformation occurred. I knew there were serious matters in my own life that had to be dealt with. I encountered a number of young poets, one of whom was John Sutherland, but not *the* John Sutherland. The first one was one of the most remarkable men I've ever known. He taught me an enormous amount about poetry, along with several other people, some of whom have been published. They were all Marxists, radicals of one kind or another. I began to write more serious poetry when I came to university. I have a manuscript of that which has never been published. I was widely published in college magazines under a series of pseudonyms.

Interviewers: What were they?

Mandel: One was Peter Wolff. He might go back to 1942. These poems would be still available in the old magazines. I might have published twenty or thirty altogether. Another name was Iago and there was Ishmael because he was a wild ass of a man! That's the history of the early poetry. Then I wrote the "Minotaur Poems" while still at college.

Interviewers: How did your first book-form publication, *Trio*, come about?

Mandel: Well, that's a real story. One of the early poems I wrote as a college student was called "Train Wreck", which was actually written on a train. There were four of us: John Edmonds, Blair Neatby, Mel Newman and myself—all going from the West to Toronto to be interviewed by a very distinguished scholarship committee. It would allow one of us to go to Britain or Europe to study. Blair Neatby won. The committee consisted of people like Cyril James, Sidney Smith, Vincent Massey, Roland Mitchener and a couple of others of the same merit. On that train, with the assistance of the other three, I wrote this poem called "Train Wreck". It was published in *Northern Review*, which was edited by *the* John Sutherland. It was the first poem I ever had published in a formal, literary journal. When I came to Toronto sometime later, Ray Souster phoned me and said: "I saw your poem in *Northern Review*: have you got any other poems?" This is the way things happen in the literary world. So I sent him some and he published them in his magazine *Contact*. He invited me over to dinner and we talked about Dudek and Layton and other people I'd never heard of before. A couple of weeks later, Ray phoned again and said, "Have you got enough poetry around for a manuscript?" I said "yes". He replied, "Send it to me. We've got a chance to publish it." And sure enough, six weeks later he called and said, "Hey man, you're in." He said they had enough money from the Social Science Research Council to publish the book, but it was really Frank Scott who was bankrolling the project. So Louis Dudek and Ray Souster published Gael Turnbull, Phyllis Webb and myself in a little book called *Trio*. That's how it all happened. That was an enormous breakthrough. I was very lucky.

Interviewers: Louis Dudek said in his introduction to *Trio* that the poetry in that volume marked a shift away from the mainstream of Canadian poetry in that it was focussed on the mythic and the fanciful aspects of experience rather than the socially relevant. Do you feel that this was really happening at that time?

Mandel: I don't know. I think someday somebody will have to sort out what really happened during that period. Was there a shift from social to mythic poetry? Or was it only a slight alteration in perspective? My own preference is to say that the poetry of the Fifties, which includes Douglas LePan, Jay Macpherson, James Reaney, Wilfred Watson, Anne Wilkinson, P.K. Page and so on, is, as Frye would have it, a mythopoeic poetry age. It was the great age of mythopoeia. But there was nothing startling about that because the whole culture was involved in that enormous imaginative endeavour. The whole movement was influenced by the mythopoeic age in which the poets were writing and not, as is popularly thought, by Northrop Frye. Yeats, Eliot, Pound and Joyce were influences. As Frye argued, the whole modern age was mythopoeic. What one was hearing in our voices was an awareness of that mythopoeia rather than some alteration of emphasis. Frye was commenting on it, giving it validity.

Interviewers: Did you take any courses with Frye while you were doing your Ph.D. at the University of Toronto?

Mandel: No, I didn't take courses, but he was one of the readers of my thesis. All my poems in *Trio* were already written by the time I read and met Frye.

Interviewers: You wrote your thesis on the eighteenth-century eccentric, religious poet, Christopher Smart. Do you see any connection between your work and his?

Mandel: It is astonishing how little I've absorbed and assimilated his work. I've been utterly devastated by my inability to do this. You understand that Smart has been an influence on b p nichol. This can be seen particularly in nichol's "sweet jesus lunatic", the title of which is taken from Smart. Robert Kroetsch has written an alphabet poem, "The Sad Phoenician", which is clearly derived from the kind of alphabet construction of Smart's *Jubilate Agno*. My attempt to deal with Smart has been emotional and blurred and inept. I don't know why that is. Intellectually I grasp him, but poetically he never became anything for me at all. My *Mary Midnight* play is interesting. It is not a play really, but rather it is a poem and a version of street theatre. I think it touches on certain aspects of Smart which most people aren't aware of—the transvestism, the street-theatre aspects, the wildness of Smart and his grotesqueness. That's the kind of poetry of his that wasn't very well known at all compared to his high odes.

Interviewers: Could you explain briefly about the group of people who were published in Reaney's magazine, *Alphabet*, during the early Sixties? Were they drawn to that magazine because of a formally agreed upon literary ideology?

Mandel: I don't think so, although Reaney has the capacity to draw people to him. I may be wrong about this, but I was talking to Peggy Atwood recently and she said did I not remember when I first met her. I said I thought we met when you came to Glendon. And she said no, it was at McMaster University and it was Jay Macpherson who introduced her to me. I think there was a direct line involved in terms of the fact that Jay taught Peggy and Jay was very much a part of the tradition you are talking about, and, in turn, James Reaney was a tremendous influence on Jay Macpherson. I have in front of me Macpherson's latest book, *The Spirit of Solitude: Conventions and Continuities in Late Romance*. Well, that was Atwood's Ph.D. thesis topic. This could well have been Margaret Atwood's book. That says something about the continuities among this group. Reaney is perpetuating the grand myth, or rather fiction, of Canadian writing concerning these moments where everything was suddenly transformed. I can remember nights when we stayed up all night reading Frye's *Fearful Symmetry*, talking about the "fall", and the moon as a distant spectre, and the whole world was being transformed by what we were doing. There's a kind of evangelical fervour to the editorial in the first *Alphabet* which I think is part of the whole thing. Reaney certainly thought that the magazine would transform consciousness in this country, and, to a degree, I think it has.

Interviewers: In the words of the poets who appeared in *Alphabet*, there were strong elements of the 'gothic'. What do you think accounts for this?

Mandel: Well, to me, the gothic is not just the lonely wanderer in the wood or the fall into time and space, and not simply the quest for the self. It's the form the quest for self takes. The form of the quest for the self can become a gothic form and when it becomes that it becomes the myth of Narcissus and of Echo, and one aspect of that becomes a demonic figure. Also, we have the double who becomes a demonic figure and manifests itself in a gothic tale such as the story of Jekyll and Hyde or in the true gothic story itself. It's because the conventions of romanticism develop into the conventions of gothic that romantic writers who are engaged in the 'family romance' at the beginning in Canada end up, I think, as gothic writers. And that's one of the major themes of Canadian writing. These writers are working out here the structure of Canadian writing. And they were all doing this simultaneously and quite independently.

Interviewers: And this strain of gothic in Canadian writing, particularly in the late Fifties and early Sixties seems to be peculiar to Toronto writers who were at the University of Toronto during that period...

Mandel: You're touching on a very profound question. On the one hand only some of the people from that time are concerned with the gothic. Frye, for instance, is not really concerned about the gothic. He's concerned with the larger issue of Romanticism in general—the Blakean dimensions of Romanticism.

Interviewers: The comic?

Mandel: Yes, the comic. That's a good point. I think Macpherson and Atwood are concerned with the gothic.

Interviewers: It is very strong in Reaney.

Mandel: Yes, Reaney and French Canadian writers like Anne Hébert and Marie-Claire Blais. It is also strong in Kroetsch. It is better to think of my own work as being gothic in its interests, rather than mythic. For instance, with my theme of the family romance, the grotesque situation we find ourselves in as writers in this country—the culture itself is involved in this, not just some professors who had some notions about the gothic.

Interviewers: Does the strongly regional nature of Canadian writing also account for this gothic strain? It certainly seems to in the U.S., the works of Hawthorne and Faulkner come to mind.

Mandel: Yes, I would agree with that. The closed-in aspects of the regional situation, the way in which a writer feels himself to be closed in by the society around him produces distortions. Peculiarities occur.

Interviewers: You seem to have deliberately cultivated a low public profile, but yet you seem to be very attracted to writers such as Layton, Smart, etc., who used their high public profiles as a way of getting their message across, of seeking a wider readership. Could you comment on this?

Mandel: That's very intriguing. (Laughter.) I thought you would have said Christopher Dewdney instead of Christopher Smart. (Laughter.) I think the answer to that question is that you are talking about doubles. The one aspect of Eli Mandel is the figure who thinks, writes, who wants to be by himself, who is appalled by the whole public aspect of the art. There's the other aspect, though, that is the double side— which is Irving Layton. I've been very close to Irving for over thirty-five years. So I think that would be my answer—that Irving Layton is my double. (Laughter.)

Interviewers: Could you comment on the notion of heroism, literary or otherwise?

Mandel: James Agee is one of my heroes. I was totally stunned when I was first introduced to Agee's work by W.O. Mitchell's son, who was a student of mine. I guess it was Agee's phenomenology that attracted me. I think John Berryman has been another one of my heroes. The romantic desperation of a whole vast number of figures in American culture, the Savage God theme in A. Alvarez, has struck me so that I find I am moved by people in pop art like Janis Joplin and Jimi Hendrix. I can't handle pop-art very well so I don't say much about that. Judy Garland—she's very important to me, especially very early in my life. As she grew into her desperation she became more important to me. Saul Bellow, in his book, *Humboldt's Gift*, writes about the American hero who writes himself out of existence—a Delmore Schwartz kind of thing. That's my hero.

Interviewers: Are they examples for you or icons?

Mandel: Well, they're not exactly icons. I should say that I did begin my poetry with the belief that poetry was the illness that made man well. The poet was the man who paid the price. I got that from reading Thomas Mann, from his Nietszchean view and Freudian view of what the situation was. I think that's where I began. So what happens then when you begin a poetics that says it is the poet's sickness that makes society well? What happens when you become well? The answer is Freud's answer—it is one of the great humanist answers ever given—Freud said essentially that you never get cured of your illness. All that happens is that you come to terms with it, until you can finally live with it. In other words, eventually you do not suffer from illness, but only what everyone else suffers from. It is not quite distancing.

Interviewers: It is readjustment.

Mandel: Yes, precisely.

Interviewers: You've often written about the *dopplegänger*, the double...

Mandel: Oh yes. The double seems to me to be central to my writing. I must say that was an experience when the double appeared to me in *Out of Place*. That was not thought, that was a thing that happened. You see I did actually see my double. I saw him at Banff at the "Cave and Basin", which is a wonderful place because it is on Sulphur Mountain, of all places, with the smell of sulphur and all the rest. I was at the side of the pool. My wife and kids were swimming. I looked across the pool and there was this kind of balustrade. I saw this man walk across and stop and lean and wave over at me.

It was myself. I was absolutely stunned by this. I didn't think about it. I had no theories or notions about the double. It took me about six months before I began to write about the thing. I tried to write about it, but I romanticized it and then I got the notion about writing it when I was in Banff a year later. The notion came to me because in the meantime, I had read the comments of Jorge Luis Borges. In the cultures of all people the double is an omen of death. It is a demonic omen. But Borges said it is an omen of death to all cultures expect the Jews. For Jews, the double is an omen of the immediate onset of prophetic powers. It was when I read that that I understood then that the onset of prophetic powers had something to do with the book I was writing. I felt I had to work the double into my book. And of course that book was *Out of Place*. My mind was structurally working out a problem, that poetically it was trying to solve—the anxiety caused by facing the problem probably created the double. The answer was being granted to me by my own mind. But my own mind was saying that what you have to do is to split yourself in two. I decided I had to do an anatomy of the double in order to understand what "out of place" meant.

Interviewers: Travelling provided you the opportunity to experience the double.

Mandel: Travel for me is being where one does not belong. Travel was the source of the enormous anxiety which underlies *Life Sentence* and *Out of Place*. That anxiety was the generating power of the poetry. Astonishingly, going away takes you back to where you are going from and that generates poetry for me. I think that is a particularly Canadian situation. Birney, Purdy, Pat Lane all work out of the travel situation.

Interviewers: Is literature a continuum?

Mandel: Oh yes. It is the awful continuum of our lives. It is the way in which one articulates oneself as a human being. It is a continuum and therefore a problem. It is a continuum but you don't like it because it is a source of anxiety, because it is a perpetual manifestation of your failure to achieve, of your not having conquered your father, of being subject to your father, all those ancestors. One of the great realizations of recent Canadian poetry is that we have ancestors. Once we were haunted by our lack of ghosts, but no longer. There are plenty of ghosts there now.

Interviewers: So there's no real way we can stop reiterating our problems.

Mandel: That's exactly it. It's a labyrinth.

Milton Acorn

In the Cause of the Working-Class

Sitting adjacent to the pile of flophouse-type mattresses, two men huddled in long winter coats. They stared through the streaking white light of the lobby as we approached the desk clerk.

Interviewers: Milton Acorn here?

Desk Clerk: Acorn? Acorn?

Interviewers: We were told...

Desk Clerk: Oh, I know who you mean—the Professor. Yeah, he's here. His friend said he'd be down to meet you.

The elevator doors wheezed open and out walked Toronto poet, James Deahl, one of the people to whom Acorn dedicated his book *Dig Up My Heart.* He led us up to Acorn's room.

Deahl: Here's the room. I'll just come in for a minute to say goodbye to Milton. He's flying out tonight to P.E.I.

It was a large, yellow-walled, bed-sitting room, full of cigar smoke, books on astronomy and poetry manuscripts. A single large window looked out on Toronto's Kensington Market. Milton Acorn sat by the window, jawing on a burnt-out cigar stub. Acorn and Deahl said their goodbyes, and then Deahl introduced us.

Interviewers: In your recent work, *Captain Neal MacDougall and the Naked Goddess,* the reader is asked to accept MacDougall as an actual real-life character...

Acorn: Yes, he wrote poetry you know. He was my great-grandfather. You see any man who makes a great impression eventually gets celebrated in poetry.

Interviewers: One of the sonnets you wrote in the *MacDougall* book was written, you've said, in a very short space of time. It was almost as if it had been dictated to you by some supernatural force.

Acorn: Yes, there's no doubt there are psychic influences around of many kinds. This world is very old and the universe is much older. We have been invaded by foreign influences many times. It was almost a voice that came to me, you know. I'd hear him talking. Sort of in my head. There's a voice in my head. My forte has been the "jackpine sonnet", which has more or less lines than fourteen, but the five sonnets in my book have fourteen lines because the Captain insisted on it. Only by cutting him off suddenly and abruptly could I ever trick him out of it. In some poems, several voices meet until one emerges. Many times I discover a voice in a poem which previously I thought was my own creation. The most incredible incident was the creation of Martin Dorion. I went up to Perth County or somewhere around there and we (Dorion and myself) recorded these poems. I won't go through all the strange things that went on. When I heard the poems, it wasn't me at all! You see I'm a second tenor usually, but this was first tenor. And a very tough voice. I identified the muse as an Acadian. There's some Acadian in me, you know. There are a great number of poems written around this voice, which I entitled Martin Dorian.

Interviewers: It's interesting that all the voices are good Prince Edward Islanders.

Acorn: Are they? (Laughter.)

Interviewers: Do you find that Prince Edward Islanders are more open to the acceptance of supernatural phenomena?

Acorn: I'd say that's a quality of rural Canada in general. Sometimes the voices will come to me in a visionary state but mostly they're just in my head. In some cases, where the poems have been dictated, I've felt as if some powerful spirit had come into the room and said: "Take a letter". (Laughter.) Some of these visitations by the force led to the exposure of until-then-hidden aspects of MacDougall's life. His nickname was 'Daddy' and it came out in that poem that he had been a smuggler in his youth. This was a guy, you know, who was supposed to have been a very respectable pillar of the community and all. But in the early days of Prince Edward Island, smuggling was respectable. It was respectable because it bypassed the inquisitions of the colonial powers in North America.

Interviewers: When you were growing up, was there encouragement from your family for your artistic endeavours?

Acorn: No one made much of it. It is a general Prince Edward Island thing to sit around thinking up songs, generally bawdy versions of old songs.

Interviewers: But you went to the trouble of writing them down?

Acorn: Yes, from about the age of four.

Interviewers: What did the other members of the family think of your artistic pursuits?

Acorn: Oh, my poor Dad thought my imagination would drive me crazy. My Dad was a real story-teller. Truth and fantasy. He would talk about his experiences in the war and all of a sudden would wander off into complete fantasy. Yet he was afraid that *my* imagination would lead me to madness. Of course, you know, it's not true at all. The repression of imagination is what leads to madness.

Interviewers: Your brother was influential wasn't he?

Acorn: Oh yes. He taught me how to scan. Iambic pentameter, you know, which has always been basic to many of my poems. Many of my short lines, for instance, are simply iambic lines broken in two!

Interviewers: Wasn't your grandfather a writer of sorts as well?

Acorn: Yes. He wrote a response to a very official version of Prince Edward Island's history. He contradicted as much of it as he could. The whole pamphlet has disappeared, but, oh well, it will turn up again someday. My grandfather was the son-in-law of Captain Neal MacDougall. He was a man of mystery—erased from the history books. All his papers, that I went over as a young boy were on topics like "Class Struggle and Equality", "Class Struggle and the Tourist Question". (Laughter.)

Interviewers: Did these help to form some of your political opinions?

Acorn: I didn't get it at the time, but it formed my mind. It set the terms in which I thought.

Interviewers: Aren't all your relatives like that—like the one involved in the Paris Commune of 1870?

Acorn: Well, he did something during that time, but I've romanticized that a lot—can't find any basis for it, you know. I've read and read about this time and found one very naughty and nutty story. Julian Huxley was giving a lecture in Oxford on the 'Missing Link' and a trap door opened in the ceiling of the hall and someone let down a dummy of a grotesque-looking ape with the sign on it, "The Missing Link". I remember that from my grandfather's stories because he was the man on the other end of the rope.

Interviewers: Could you talk a bit about your wartime experiences?

Acorn: I was a spectator, but they shot me anyway! That's the best summation. It was a very hard and embarrassing time.

Interviewers: That's when the depth-charge gave you a concussion?

Acorn: That's right. It drove me completely cuckoo. I refused to die, though. I even fought to rally myself and get back in the active service again. Finally, I said to the doctor: "Send me to active service or send me home". They sent me home.

Interviewers: How exactly did the concussion happen?

Acorn: It was a blast, just a pure blast. I didn't have enough sense to cover my ears. Typical story of the young intellectual. I should have been an officer, but they made me a sergeant instead and there was no one behind me to say "Put your hands over your ears". I looked at the depth charge and said to myself: "The blast from that charge is going to reach me in nineteen seconds," so I started counting but never thought to put my hands over my ears. It happened while I was standing on a troop-ship going over to England. The nervousness of the Canadians in that situation was just incredible. It was a near-death experience. There's lots of things I'm terribly afraid of now, but not death.

Interviewers: When you came back, you went to Montreal and became a political activist.

Acorn: Yes, I had been in the Canadian army, fighting against the same enemy that Joe Stalin was fighting against. Just after that there was a lot of anti-Stalin propaganda, and, I thought, there must be something to this or else they wouldn't be putting on such a show against him. All the time I was taking my carpentry course I couldn't do things right because my mind was always thinking, always thinking, saying "communism is right, communism is right". There was a strike on in the town, then, and it was odd how my mates just couldn't get the political implications. They were all for the workers, of course, but when it came to a vote they voted for the man who broke the strike.

Interviewers: What originally attracted you to politics?

Acorn: I just had the URGE, URGE, URGE! I didn't even bother with sex! My first driving urge was to get into political action. They were driving all the communists out of town, but they didn't touch me, of course—old family and all that, lots of relatives and I was a tremendously strong man. If someone had told me to get out of town, I would have thrown him in the direction of Nova Scotia.

Acorn: Could you talk about your days in Montreal after the war?

Acorn: I couldn't get very much carpentry work, because I didn't speak French very well. I could speak French mainly for jokes, mostly a queer language I'd made up myself.

Interviewers: You met Layton in Montreal?

Acorn: Yes, I met Layton. I went to his house one day with a bundle of poems. He read them and was quite delighted. But somehow I didn't exactly take to him. Nobody could. He didn't have enough charity. He could have been saved if he had had a certain amount of charity.

Interviewers: Did the ideology get in the way?

Acorn: He was pro-Soviet at that time, but his idea of communism was crazy! Crazy! He thought that communism was a concept of an elite.

Interviewers: You also met Al Purdy in Montreal.

Acorn: Yeah, Layton sent me down to him with some poems. I wanted to write some plays and Layton said Purdy was doing the same. I walked in the door and Purdy immediately wanted to talk about communism. I didn't satisfy him much. We agreed for many years, but there were too many ifs, ands, buts and maybes in my concept of communism. I would speak in the bluntest aphorisms you've ever heard and he'd give twenty-paragraph propositions which I would answer in five words or less.

Interviewers: You helped him build his house at Ameliasburg.

Acorn: Oh yes. I couldn't persuade him, couldn't persuade him that a rafter had a top and a bottom. Every time I turned around he had the rafter in wrong. (Laughter.) We would battle and dispute constantly. Battle and dispute all the way. It took us two days to lay a line of rafters across one room. It was very irritating. It was a question of my patience and Purdy's impatience. We always got on for many years. In fact, he's the editor of my book, *Dig Up My Heart.* My memories of our relationship are frustration—I love the guy but he's always refusing to agree with me! He never let a question drop. I'd say, okay we'd agree to disagree and he'd say "No! No!" And then you'd bring up a question about ethics and he'd go: "Why discuss ethics. Is there a God?" Well, you either know there is a God or you don't know. I always think there's some sort of spiritual influence. As I've studied science, I've become more and more convinced, the universe was cooked in one pot. It's obvious. I mean, as far as the eye can see or telescopes can detect, the universe is all of one piece—a canasta deck of ninety-odd elements. They're all made of the same mix. The universe is made. It had to be made.

Interviewers: How do you reconcile your belief in this creator God with your belief in an atheistic doctrine like communism?

Acorn: Well, Marx is no help. His denunciation of religion is such a perplexing problem that it is almost half a defence of religion. I see things, not in an orthodox religious sense, but in an infinite sense.

Interviewers: I've Tasted My Blood wasn't awarded the Governor-General's Award in 1970, but there was instead the famous evening at Grossman's Tavern when a group of poets awarded you the "People's Poet Award".

Acorn: The American poet, Carl Sandburg, had just died and he'd had that title and I guess they declared I should inherit his mantle.

Interviewers: What do you remember about that evening?

Acorn: There were seven fights! A fellow came up to Purdy and made one or two remarks and Purdy sort of badgered him and the fellow said: "Oh, fuck off." And Purdy said: "Oh, you fuck off", and Purdy picked him up and threw him, at which point he was caught by the waiters and thrown the rest of the way out.

Interviewers: What directions do you feel poetry is taking now?

Acorn: Definitely back to the lyric. There are some fine poets, such as George Johnston, who have maintained the lyric all along. The "jackpine sonnet", for instance, that I invented, has that lyrical form.

Interviewers: What made you arrive at the name and form of the jackpine sonnet?

Acorn: It is the irregularity of it. I like jackpines. It is a very Canadian tree. The sonnet is meant to be heard—by the masses. It is a spoken form. My poetry speaks to the most essential question—the cause of the working-class. The rupture between the petit-bourgeoisie and the working-class on the question of poetry is now complete. Workers like music in language. They don't take to this sour-porridge style at all. A lot of modern poetry sets up a barrier of language between the poet and the people. You will notice that I write for the working-class—my poems are for ordinary people.

Interviewers: But your poems also touch on other social issues, such as abortion.

Acorn: Abortion is a regressive policy. It is so utterly against the spirit of Marx. What I mean by that is that, under Stalin, for instance, abortion in the Soviet Union was only allowed in specific physical health circumstances. Two doctors had to be called in for consultation in a case. One of the first things the revisionist regime did after Stalin was to permit abortion on demand and their line was they'd permit it but not encourage it. This had a tremendously demoralizing effect on society.

Interviewers: How do you address social issues without being preachy, pedantic...

Acorn: Social issues have to be addressed in poetry, but in a style and language that is comprehensible. If the working-classes can't understand you, then you are ultimately incomprehensible. I stand on the side of the working-class, so I will always be understood. That's a good feeling to have.

Al Purdy

The Phony, the Realistic and the Genuine

It was an uncomfortably hot day in mid-July as we drove through Prince Edward County, which statistically has the lowest alcohol consumption rate in the province of Ontario. It is a country of sand dunes, parched farms and an incredibly wide variety of lawn ornaments, chiefly featuring lawn-jockeys, flamingos, elves and wind-mobilized smurfs. We followed a maze of dusty roads to the town of Ameliasburg, where a child on a tricycle parked in front of Owen Roblin's octagonal house (a landmark in the poetry of Al Purdy) directed us over the bridge and down the hill to a blue-roofed A-frame house, where an apparently heat-exhausted seagull flopped about on the lawn.

　　We arrived just as Al Purdy and George Galt (a writer for *Saturday Night* and other publications) were finishing lunch. Purdy's wife, Eurithe, was attempting to clear the cluttered table of several bottles of wine, U.S.-made Canadian beer and paté and bread. Purdy's large kitchen window looked out on Roblin Lake toward Ameliasburg. In the distance, above the trees, rose the steeple of the town church, which figures prominently in Purdy's poem "Wilderness Gothic". The lake itself, an important landmark and reference point in Purdy's work, lay calm and reflecting in the afternoon sun.

Alfred Wellington Purdy was born in Wooler, Ontario in 1918 and received his education in Trenton and Belleville before working at a series of jobs that took him across Canada. He won the Governor-General's Award for Poetry in 1965 for *Cariboo Horses*.

Galt: So, how did you guys get to interview Leonard Cohen, anyway?

Purdy: You must have known his girlfriend.

Interviewers: We got his number from Irving Layton.

Purdy: Oh, I see. From Layton.

Interviewers: How do you feel about Layton these days?

Purdy: Well, you know, when I admired Layton the most, and I mean one hundred and fifty percent, I was really incapable of knowing him. When you admire someone a lot you can't get to know them very well. I still admire Layton in many ways but you have to distance somebody to know them a little bit better. Layton is so full of shit and such a genius at the same time. I mean, what do you say about him? He's all his opposites. I was in awe of him.

Interviewers: You were also apparently in awe of Malcolm Lowry. We're referring to your piece on him in *No Other Country*.

Purdy: Oh? (Exit Galt.)

Interviewers: It seems you had a vision of him that was undercut by what you saw in real life.

Purdy: I've never been able to read *Under the Volcano*. I've read at it. I get ten pages further each year. I've reached page one hundred or so. I can't read it. I've given up on it—to hell with it! I read *The Forest Path to the Spring*. I think it is great. What I wanted to bring out in that piece on Lowry was that he was a brilliant poet as well as a novelist. I mean, the poems are very stilted, awkward and so on and their language isn't natural at all. But they are still great so I remember him for his poetry, not for his long convoluted sentences. He's the exact opposite of Hemingway, which is not to say that I love and admire Hemingway—I think he's revolting in some ways—but he's too dead accurate although he was innovative. I was, as I look back on Lowry's character, fascinated by him, particularly as I look back and see what happened to him.

Interviewers: How did you meet Lowry?

Purdy: When I first went to Vancouver in 1950, I got involved in a science-fiction club. I wrote poems and they, the other members, wrote and read science fiction and all that shit. One of the kids involved in the club was Curt Lang and Curt Lang was one of those kid geniuses of about fourteen or fifteen years of age who could talk the pants off a theologian. I've known a couple of kids like that—later on they settle down and become normal human beings of average intelligence— but at the time they awe you. Curt was one of those. He wrote a few poems for the *Canadian Forum*. Curt knew Downie Kirk who had translated Lowry into French. Curt had been a high-school student of Kirk's. Anyways, one day he said we should all go over and see Malcolm Lowry and we did.

Interviewers: It seemed during that incident, where he insisted on going into that church as a wedding was in progress, that you were totally oblivious to everyone around you except for Lowry.

Purdy: Oh yes, that's true. I was completely concentrating on him. He brushed past the wedding guests and simply knelt in the middle of the aisle of the church with these paper bags containing six bottles of Bols gin. It struck me that they were his albatross, and of course, they were. At the time I had the

albatross in my stomach and not around my neck. Do you
want another beer with me? (Laughter.)

Interviewers: Sure. Where did you get these anyway?

Purdy: You mean these American Black Labels?

Interviewers: Yeah.

Purdy: In Watertown. (Re-enter Galt.)

Galt: Are those in short supply?

Purdy: Nope.

Galt: I think I'll have one.

Purdy: I think you'll need an opener. George, find me an
opener over there.

Interviewers: You've revised many of your poems, particularly
"Elegy for a Grandfather", which has about ten different
versions.

Purdy: I might have had feelings about him, affection even,
but I could never be very close to him since he was a ferocious
old man. One of the reasons I revise is that for some reason or
other if I have to copy a poem I'll say to myself "Change this,"
or "I don't like that," or "I could do better than that,"
because poems are such a mixture of the phony, the realistic
and the genuine. When you look back on them you recognize
the phony, the realistic and the genuine.

Interviewers: You've written some poems about your father,
who died when you were quite young. But with the exception
of "Evergreen Cemetery," you haven't written many about
your mother.

Purdy: My mother was a religious fanatic. She carried it as far
as it could go. She was United Church.

Interviewers: Did this feeling about her religion influence your
rebellion against the church? (Exit Galt.)

Purdy: Only with one part of your mind could you call it
rebellion. I think that I looked at the proofs for and against

belief in God and decided against. At one time in our lives we believe that there's some God up in the sky who can see us doing things like masturbating. We don't like that and we're afraid and terrified. At a certain point you believe that you need somebody to tell you what's right and what's wrong, but you later decide you've grown up and can run your own life. I'd feel the same way about God even if a God did or did not exist. You feel you want to grow up and run your own life. Don't you want to run your own life?

O'Riordan: Yeah.

Purdy: Despite God?

O'Riordan: Not despite God.

Purdy: On account of him, then?

O'Riordan: To a certain degree.

Purdy: God helps you run your own life then?

O'Riordan: There's a certain guidance there.

Purdy: If there's a guidance you aren't really running your own life. You gotta grow up. That's what I'm trying to say. Feebly. I mean, if someone has greater authority than you there's an element of authority over you to order your life. Do you need a deity to aspire to any noble human objectives? Just because your parents were hypnotized by this deity, you think it has some validity?

O'Riordan: What's to say that they were hypnotized?

Purdy: You have to grow up don't you?

O'Riordan: That doesn't mean throwing out everything that they believed in—the tradition, the past and the ideas that made the past work.

Purdy: So, do you think there was a genuine God that manifested himself to them and that he was male, by the way? What did he do to prove himself?

Meyer: Gave them something to believe in, perhaps. What about your poem "The Darkness" where you talk about "the spirit of everyplace"—aren't you at least acknowledging some creative supernatural presence in the universe?

Purdy: Not at all. Not at all. This is a completely mythical concept—whether there is or is not a 'spirit of everyplace.' When you say that there is a particular feeling you can recognize in yourself, you say: If there is a spirit of everyplace, I feel this at this particular solemn time in my life when I'm outside in the middle of the night looking at stars bursting." That sort of thing. You know, you can feel that? That doesn't mean that there is or is not a God. God is unprovable. It has to be unprovable. We're all terrified of the idea of a God, of anybody knowing everything we do.

Interviewers: So it is the terror that brings out a perception of God then.

Purdy: Oh heck! I reject being afraid of something like that.

Interviewers: But you prayed once when you were lost in the woods near Sault Ste. Marie.

Purdy: Yeah, and it was the last time that I ever did that. I was terrified. I'm not religious at all in the usual sense, only in the sense that there are feelings and things in the world about which you can have a rather awestruck feeling. One of the things that gives you religious feelings is the hope that you can look at someone else and admire them and have feelings of great respect for them despite any shortcomings they might have. As you grow older you find that there are fewer and fewer of them. It is a helluva thing.

Interviewers: Let's turn to a less controversial subject—politics.

Purdy: Oh, on that, I'm not a member of the NDP. However, I would vote for them if I ever got around to voting. But even so, my vote would be governed by my opinion at any given time of what was best for the country. By the way, would you guys like some cigars? I picked them up in the States, too.

Interviewers: OK. Thanks. (Re-enter Galt.)

Purdy: George, are you going to scorn these cigars?

Galt: What are they like?

Purdy: They're American, not Cuban. (Galt takes one and puts it in his pocket.)

Meyer: You visited Cuba.

Purdy: That doesn't make me a communist.

O'Riordan: We didn't say that.

Purdy: You know, I was a real admirer of the U.S. until my visit to Cuba in 1964. Before that I thought everyone admired the U.S. and then I felt so embarrassed at my stupidity. On the other hand, the Cubans aren't perfect either.

O'Riordan: Yeah, I found that out too.

Purdy: So, overall you came back less right-wing than you were.

O'Riordan: I've never thought of myself as right-wing. Now you're being academic, trying to categorize me. You're trying to pin me down.

Purdy: Yeah? Why shouldn't I? You're trying to pin me down.

Meyer: No, no. We're just chatting with you.

Purdy: Bullshit! (Laughter.)

Interviewers: Did you see any parallels between the Canadian and the Cuban situation with regard to the U.S.?

Purdy: Oh sure. We too are a minor colony of the U.S. But what's wrong with hoping that your country will do the best it can? I'm only anti-American in the sense that I don't like their foreign policy. The U.S. State Department is trying to conquer the world, whether they know it or not. On the other hand, there are individuals who are geniuses. Not many poets though, except Robinson Jeffers. But both Russia and the U.S.—about them I'd say "a plague on both your houses." It is our resemblances to the U.S. that make our differences from them all the more striking. Russia is in many ways an evil dictatorship, but we have to live with them as well as with the U.S. We have to live with ourselves too.

Interviewers: When did you first start writing?

Purdy: I first started writing when I was thirteen and like all teenagers I was maladjusted. The first poem I wrote I wrote because I was trying to show off. I thought anyone could write a poem. It was published in the school magazine *Spotlight*.

Interviewers: Have you got a copy of it?

Purdy: I have somewhere. I have, I think, or maybe I sold it to the library at Queen's University. I don't remember what the poem was, except that it was terrible.

Galt: You never told me this.

Purdy: Does it matter? Are we out of beer again?

Purdy: Why don't you get more of George into this? (Exit Purdy.)

Interviewers: OK. So, George, how did you come to interview Al?

Galt: Well, Al had been kind enough to include me in that anthology he edited which featured new young Canadian poets—*Storm Warning*. And so, we corresponded. I knew we had something in common because he put in as many or more of my poems than anyone else's. (Re-enter Purdy.)

Purdy: It's hot as blazes out there, must be a hundred degrees.

Galt: Where's your bust of D.H. Lawrence?

Purdy: Eurithe has hidden it away some place. But wait a second, maybe I can find it.

Galt: You have to realize that Lawrence is one of Al's great literary loves. He has a large collection of signed first editions by Lawrence.

Purdy: Found it. (Sits down with bust and puts a beer bottle to the lips of it.) How are you going to write this up? It can't be a matter of direct question and answer.

Galt: I should show them the interview I did with you.

Purdy: That was a long time ago.

Galt: I'm glad to be part of your pension fund.

Meyer: That bust doesn't look like D.H. Lawrence. The eyes are too close together.

Purdy: It looks a helluva lot more like D.H. Lawrence than I look like Al Purdy.

Galt: That's a great line. That's a profound line.

Purdy: I think so, too. (Laughter.) But thank you.

Galt: The trouble between you and me is that we think we're too profound.

Purdy: No! I don't think we're profound. I think you write well but I don't think you're profound.

Galt: What's the difference?

Purdy: I don't think I want to go into it now. I don't think either of us wants to be profound. I almost always tell the truth unless I want to impress somebody. Can you guys tell when I'm telling the truth?

Meyer: What do you think, George?

Galt: Has anyone got a good cigar? (Exit Galt.)

Interviewers: You've travelled a great deal. Many of your poems are about places outside Canada. Has travelling influenced your perception?

Purdy: One becomes presumably more objective about Canada. One sees the country's virtues and defects more clearly by comparing it with other nations. However, I don't travel for such reasons. My motives are to shake myself out of lethargy, to be stimulated in both thought and action. And to write, which derives something from such stimulation.

Interviewers: Some places you have been must have stood out from others. What are your favourite places?

Purdy: Favourite places? The B.C. mountains, Machu Picchu and Cuzco, Greece, Turkey and the Canadian Arctic...

Interviewers: About the Arctic, you collaborated on a book with A.Y. Jackson called *North of Summer.*

Purdy: Not really. I didn't actually collaborate with Jackson. I didn't see him in the Arctic at all. It seems like a collaboration because my publisher thought it was good to use his sketches. I had to go to the Arctic in order to write about it. Touch, sight, smell mean much more than just reading about places in books. I was, perhaps, a little frightened by the idea of endless snow and very cold temperatures. I was careful to go there in summer. Perhaps I wanted to see how I felt about frightening things at close range. I had, of course, read about the Arctic. But it was never the same as sight, touch, sound and smell. I suppose those things have been a large part of my education.

Interviewers: You seem to have stayed away from many of the poetry movements in Canada.

Purdy: I was never central in any, always peripheral, and only peripheral because of the people. I don't like movements as such. Obviously some writers need the stimulation of being close to other writers. I don't. Writers begin to bore me after a short period, all those egos jostling together. Of course, I've been influenced by other writers, early on by Layton, especially. But I've been influenced by so many people that I don't regard this as influence. One takes it into one's self. Among them, Lawrence especially, and quite a bit from him in the last twenty years. Before that there were so many—Bliss Carman, Dylan Thomas, Chesterton, the Black Mountain Boys—I wanted to be opposite them and yet I learned from them. Also Jeffers counts as an influence. It is interesting that Lawrence learned from Whitman but I was never attracted to Whitman's poetry for some reason.

Interviewers: How about Dudek whom you knew in Montreal?

Purdy: Well, Layton and Dudek were friendly at one time but there was always an undercurrent between them, something that was difficult to put your finger on. I don't know how their quarrel started—possibly Dudek's belief in the Pound-Williams way of writing and Irving's somewhat wider spectrum.

Interviewers: Will you continue to write poetry?

Purdy: You write what you're able to write even if that fails. My longest dry spell was some five years. Not that I didn't write things that weren't too bad. But you always realize it when you are mediocre. You want to give the best of yourself. There are no excuses. You escape such barren periods by being interested in life itself.

Interviewers: How do you think you'll be remembered?

Purdy: Remembered? For the poems, the poems themselves. They replace me in my absence.

Roo Borson
Conjuring Something New

Timothy Findley met Roo Borson while she was a physics technician at the University of Toronto. He was impressed with her quiet but self-confident manner and with a day-to-day involvement in a completely non-literary field. He recommended that we interview her, not only because she was representative of a new generation of Canadian poets, but because he was struck by the fact that an American had adapted to Canada and the Canadian literary scene in such a thorough way. She agreed to meet us in a quiet upper room of Hart House.

Born in Berkeley California in 1952, she attended Goddard College in Vermont, where she was taught by American poet Louise Glück, and the University of British Columbia, where she studied Creative Writing. She was the youngest poet to be included in Margaret Atwood's *New Oxford Book of Canadian Verse* and William Toye's *Oxford Companion to Canadian Literature*. She is the author of four books of poetry.

Interviewers: You've written four books so far. Which of them has been the most satisfying for you?

Borson: A Sad Device is the best one by far. Simply because I'm still practising and so far it represents the highest stage of my practising.

Interviewers: We noticed that many of the poems can be dated back several years, into the Seventies. Was A Sad Device a long time in preparation?

Borson: That lag between composition and publication can be accounted for by the fact that it takes a while to put together a manuscript and once you have it you send it around to publishers and it takes a while before someone accepts it. The manuscript of A Sad Device was rejected by three publishers. The way it got published was that Gary Geddes at Quadrant Editions wrote and asked if I had any manuscripts and I sent him A Sad Device.

Interviewers: Could you comment on the significance of the cover of A Sad Device?

Borson: I didn't choose it. (Laughter.) Gary Geddes wrote and said he had a great picture for the cover, but I didn't see it until I got the copies of the book. I like it quite a bit. I've had a few complaints about the photo on the back, which I also like quite a bit. The cover makes sense to me because, well, what I tell people is that it is a photograph of me on a bad day. It is a head that's a lit lamp, out searching—it's a mechanical sad device, sometimes with a light in it, sometimes not.

Interviewers: Could you talk about the manuscript you are working on now?

Borson: It is set in California where I grew up. Some of it is from memory, some of it made up. Some of it is from visiting that place again. What identifies it as Californian is the landscape—the water, the trees, the hills. It will be in two parts. The first part consists of verse poems and the second part contains prose poems, which is a new way of writing for me.

Interviewers: What are the difficulties in writing a prose poem as opposed to a verse poem?

Borson: They are just two totally different media. Prose poems are not short stories, but they aren't poems either. There's something different in terms of rhythmic flow. Instead of having thought or idea-breaks at the end of lines, you have something less compact but more dramatic.

Interviewers: It is interesting that the book deals with your childhood landscape of California. Are there any significant events that stand out for you from your childhood?

Borson: Not really events, but images. The poems that I first wrote for this book are the traditional line-length poems, and they are not about events when growing up but rather about what teenagers are like. It is not actually very personal. It is very much about other people. The poems are attempting to evoke feelings about that time in life. In the prose poems there is a tendency to go further back into early childhood, which is more personal because my actual parents are there in the poetry. In some ways the prose poems are often character sketches.

Interviewers: Do you think poets are going back to a more narrative form of verse in order to deal with such subjects as their "roots"?

Borson: Poetry in general is becoming more narrative at this point in time, and that includes characterization and long lines and a more colloquial rhetoric.

Interviewers: When did you first start writing? Was there a particular moment when you knew that you were a poet?

Borson: I guess it is the difference between when I became an artist and when I became a poet, as opposed to a musician, a potter, a craftsperson. I became an artist when I was four years old and suddenly became conscious of the room around me in a way I hadn't before. I have hardly any memories before that certain day when I was four. I knew in some intuitive sense, at that time, what my vocation was but I didn't know what to do with it. As far as poetry goes, I started writing little lyrics as soon as I learned how to speak and write. Probably, through accidents, I settled into poetry as opposed to any of the other arts, and I'm still learning poetry.

Interviewers: Do you still practice any of the other arts?

Borson: No, poetry and just plain living take up all my time.

Interviewers: What were the major influences on your poetic development?

Borson: Probably Wordsworth, who my father often quoted at the breakfast table. My father did not read very much poetry so this was an anomaly. He also quoted a bit of Shakespeare here and there. The first poets I really read were e.e. cummings and Dylan Thomas, and that was by poking around in my sister's bookcase.

Interviewers: You did your undergraduate work at Goddard College in Vermont with Louise Glück. Was she an influence on you and how would you compare your work with hers?

Borson: She writes in a stiff, East Coast manner that is extremely crafted and which I admire very much. But I'm not trying to say the kinds of things she is trying to say. She's very reserved and I don't want to be that way. She was an influence on me because she was very good and because she was a very contemporary poet. At that point it was very important for me to be around people who were writing and who were good at it because I wasn't good at it and needed to learn. I think the way to learn how to write better is to hang around people who are good and to see how they think.

Interviewers: After you finished at Goddard, you went to the University of British Columbia and studied Creative Writing. Why did you go there and who did you want to study with?

Borson: I went to UBC because I was living in Vancouver at the time and I had a job at the Vancouver Public Library as a clerk. I discovered UBC existed and that they had a Creative Writing department. I thought it would be a wonderful thing to do to take courses there. At the time Pat Lowther was to teach the graduate poetry course and we had about two class meetings and then she disappeared. It was much later that it came out that she had been murdered by her husband. So then Robert Bringhurst took over the course.

Interviewers: How would you describe your creative relationship with Robert Bringhurst?

Borson: He is my teacher for all time. Although I admire Louise Glück, Robert Bringhurst has been more influential. He taught me the first leaps and bounds in craft. I'm sure he doesn't even know how he did that. The kinds of things he would say, the kinds of poets and poems he would point out as being good, suddenly caught my mind and I understood what to do.

Interviewers: Do you see youself as a West Coast writer, an expatriate American writer, a Toronto writer or do you resist these labels?

Borson: I'm a Canadian poet because I've learned most of what I know and feel about poetry since I came to Canada.

Interviewers: So your sensibility has been shaped here rather than in the U.S.?

Borson: Yes, even though I write about the U.S. occasionally. My sensibility has been shaped by Canadian poetry.

Interviewers: You've lived in many different places both in the U.S. and Canada. Where is the ideal landscape for you?

Borson: I really thrive on change and like to move back and forth as often as possible. I like all kinds of landscapes. I like Sudbury. (Laughter.) Moving around appeals to me greatly. I am really excited by physical scenery. I'm a very visually-oriented person. The beauty and newness of landscape excites me. I get tired of seeing the same old thing everyday.

Interviewers: Are there anxieties which you feel you must articulate resulting from the social upheavals of the Sixties?

Borson: I was in high school during the Viet-Nam War. All that was happening definitely influenced me at the time, and

I attended all the big rallies. I don't talk about political things in my poems because I don't think about politics very much. I think about individuals being wounded, but I don't have a head for those mass-scale happenings between nations. I wish I did. On the other hand, feminism is extremely important to me, and looking back at *A Sad Device* I see where I was using paternalistic language in writing some of those poems. I now regret that but it was a learning experience. I didn't realize how much of my own language was dictated by the fact that our language is male-oriented.

Interviewers: As somebody who has lived both in the U.S. and Canada and is in fact going back to the U.S....

Borson: Only temporarily!

Interviewers: Well, in Canada there's a lot of talk about the Canadian identity and you seem to be in a unique position to evaluate this identity. What are the essential differences between Americans and Canadians?

Borson: When I first came to Canada, which was about eight years ago, I had an image of Canada which was very fine, very pure, beautiful. A lot of my friends were draft-dodgers. Many of them came to Canada, and wound up going back to the U.S. because they couldn't deal with the changes in culture. When I arrived in Vancouver, which was the first city in Canada I lived in, I noticed a greater reserve in the people on the streets. But of course that's coming from California where strangers put their arms around each other and everyone is more expressive. I don't know what the essential differences are between Americans and Canadians. Some of the stereotypes apply. Americans, I think, are more aggressive socially and nationally. Canadians are more reserved than Americans. And so am I. But beyond those small kinds of differences, there's not much I can say. I was shocked to find out that Canadians had an "identity crisis" because I had a very strong identity for Canada even before I came here. It took quite a long time for that to wear down. It is there. I feel that Canada is a huge, beautiful, pure country that I'm very much at home in. I can't see it from the inside out, only from the outside in.

Interviewers: How does the idea for a poem crystallize for you?

Borson: For me, there are not ideas at all; simply there's some energy in me and it has got to get out. If I run around the track twenty-one times and it is not out, then I know it is a poem! It is very physical. I get quite disturbed physically and emotionally because there's something in there that doesn't know how to get out. But it is certainly not an idea.

Interviewers: How does a poem actually start then?

Borson: Well, sometimes what triggers it is just seeing a bit of physical imagery. I see something and it is beautiful and it calls up something within me. And other times when I get disturbed it is usually some interaction between people at a deep level, or some crime that has been committed in the streets, or my relationship to the world is wrong somehow and I have to work that out. It is totally unconscious.

Interviewers: How then does it progress to the conscious level?

Borson: Very fumblingly. I just spit out a lot of words on the page and I write a lot of garbage, incredible garbage. And out of that I find little bits here and there and use those together and look to see if anything can be structured out of them. As much as I try to sit down and follow a thought from beginning to end, it is just not how it works for me. I have to write reams and reams of junk to get at anything real.

Interviewers: Other than the fact that there's a lot being written, what characterizes this period in Canadian poetry?

Borson: I think there is a huge variety in what is being written. One of the things I like about poetry in Canada at this time, as opposed to poetry in the U.S., is this variety and its unpredictability. American poets are becoming very predictable in what they write about and how they write.

Interviewers: What do you think of Margaret Atwood's selection of your work for *The New Oxford Book of Canadian Verse?*

Borson: One of the poems is one of my favourites but the three others are not favourites of mine.

Interviewers: Which one was the favourite?

Borson: "Flowers". They were all taken from *A Sad Device.* I was surprised particularly by the inclusion of "Jacaranda", which has a lot of problems.

Interviewers: What were the circumstances surrounding the publication of your first book, *Landfall?*

Borson: Michael Yates who lived in Vancouver when I did phoned me up one day and said: "Roo it's time you got a book out." I said "No!" But I eventually put a manuscript together and sent it off to him and he sent it to Fred Cogswell at Fiddlehead. That's how it came about. On my own, I never would have done it at that point.

Interviewers: Do you feel that all the recent public exposure your work has received will influence your literary career?

Borson: No, it is not influencing the writing in the least. It is influencing the "career" because I never expected to have a "career" in poetry. If I make money from my works then I have much more time for writing, and that is all to the good. Writing is what I like to do, but I don't consider it a career. I've always hoped that the audience for my poetry would be as large as the work could command.

Interviewers: What are the anxieties and pressures on a young writer today?

Borson: The only anxiety and pressure, the only reality, is that you have to write well. I don't mean anxieties in terms of confronting one's own neuroses. I mean actually putting words on a page that will move another human being. That is very difficult. It is very hard to get anything that conjures something new for the reader. Communication is the magic of the new.

Photograph not available.

Sheila Watson
It's What You Say

It was the coldest night of the year in Toronto, and the downtown of the city looked more and more like the Cariboo region of the northern British Columbia interior with each degree that the temperature fell. A petite woman with short grey hair and large eyes, Sheila Watson arrived wearing a large fur coat with its collar turned up around her face.

Although she boasts neither the public persona nor the prolific output of other writers, her reputation as a novelist in the modernist school in Canada is undisputed. Born in 1909 in New Westminster, British Columbia, she was educated at the University of British Columbia and the University of Toronto where she taught briefly before moving to the University of Alberta. Now a West Coast resident again, she lives in Nanaimo with her husband, poet and Governor-General's Award winner, Wilfred Watson. Her landmark work, *The Double Hook* (1959), was followed in 1979 by the publication of *Four Stories*.

Interviewers: *The Double Hook* has established itself as a major novel. Could you talk about the process of writing it? How was it originally received by the critics and the public?

Watson: Actually it is very difficult to recall the process. Before I wrote *The Double Hook*, I had written a novel in which I hadn't solved certain technical problems, and the images in that novel came out of the experience I had in the Cariboo. These images had, in a strange way, become part of my language. I hadn't gone to the Cariboo to write about it and at that particular time I wasn't writing. I was thinking about it—not of writing something but of writing itself. Eventually I did write a novel called *Deep Hollow Creek*. I sent it to Macmillan and it came back. I was glad that it came back because I realized then that there was something wrong with it and felt that somehow or other I had to get the authorial voice out of the novel for it to say what I wanted it to say. I didn't want a voice talking about something. I wanted voices. When *The Double Hook* was published it was said that there were too many characters in it. I wasn't thinking of these figures, or whatever one calls them, as characters in the conventional sense.

Interviewers: You, for instance, list them in a kind of *dramatis personae* at the beginning.

Watson: Yes, I was thinking rather of a cry of voices—a *vox clamantis*—voices crying out in the wilderness. Something like the voices one hears in early litanies—voices reaching beyond themselves. I was thinking of a group of bodies that were virtually inarticulate and I had to make them articulate without making them *faux-semblants* so to speak. When I was thinking about *The Double Hook* I remembered the problems with the first novel. We were here in Toronto and I was teaching at a girls' private school. We lived on Admiral Road and I remember walking down past the Park Plaza Hotel along Bloor Street. The school was just opposite where the subway station is now—just off Yonge Street. I had a lot of time to think during those walks.

Interviewers: Where were you teaching?

Watson: It was the old Moulton College. The walk was the one time I had to myself, and I remember thinking on the corner just opposite the Anglican Church, "I know what I am going to do—I can hear the voices beginning."

Interviewers: And that was the moment of inception of *The Double Hook*?

Watson: Yes, that was the moment—far from the West Coast, under completely alien circumstances. I had wanted to get away from any idea of setting. Here the voices came from somewhere else. Place was important only in its relationship to them as ground. *The Double Hook* was conceived in Toronto and written in Calgary some time later. I could understand what Eliot meant when he said sometimes a poem begins with a rhythm. It was just as if I had caught the sound of voices coming and trying to say something and I was concerned. I was concerned, too, in another sort of way I suppose, with the problem of an indigenous population which had lost or was losing its own mythic structure, which had had its images destroyed, its myths interpreted for it by various missionary societies and later by anthropologists—a group intermarried or intermingled with people of other beliefs—French Catholics who had come into the West with the Hudson Bay Company, Biblical puritanical elements—all now virtually isolated from their source. All these voices echo in *The Double Hook*. I didn't want it to be an ethnic novel—not a novel about Indians or any other deprived group, but rather a novel about a number of people who had no ability to communicate because they had found little to replace the myths and rituals which might have bound them together. In a sense that is made explicit when Felix says, "I've got no words to clear a woman off my bench. No words except: Keep moving, scatter, get the hell out." Since he has some pity for the girl he resorts to fragments of the mass perhaps trying to remember the *ite* of the *ite, missa est.*

Interviewers: Fragments of the mass?

Watson: Yes. They are fragments like the scriptural fragments associated with Ara and echoing from the mouth of Coyote. There is confusion everywhere.

Interviewers: What is ritual, then?

Watson: Ritual is the organization of community. If ritual becomes the ritual of commercial ads, then that is ritual for better or for worse.

Interviewers: And ritual preserves the myths?

Watson: Yes it preserves them in their various forms.

Interviewers: Just after *The Double Hook* came out, *The Globe and Mail* published a review titled "Left Hook, Right Hook, K.O."

Watson: My response to that was simply "they've caught me." I hadn't realized that 'double hook' was a boxing term. I was thinking of a fish hook and perhaps an anchor. So how could I be angry? I just thought they'd got the better of me. What fun. I should have known.

Interviewers: Most first novels are autobiographical, but that doesn't seem to be the case with yours.

Watson: There are no biographical elements in *The Double Hook* at all. It is not based on individual people I knew well. It came out of a knowledge of people in specific circumstances. The only portrait from real life in the book is the parrot in the bar. There was such a parrot in the Ashcroft Hotel.

Interviewers: The other figures in *The Double Hook* are not drawn from life?

Watson: They are related to a ground. They are emerging from that ground.

Interviewers: Do you agree with critics who label *The Double Hook* a regional novel?

Watson: No. I've met people who grew up in the Black Forest in Germany who said it could have been written there. There is, however, a sense of place. I used my memories of the contours of the land as a map, not actual maps of the region or of the names of towns or highways.

Interviewers: Does that say something about the nature of Canadian geography in that you can't identify where you are by place but only by texture?

Watson: I think that's a very real dilemma. The texture of Ontario for instance is quite different from the texture of British Columbia. It not only looks different, it feels different.

Interviewers: Where did your interest in the mythopoeic originate?

Watson: Specifically in relation to West Coast myth? I suppose it was through reading the work of the early anthropologists —Franz Boas and James Teit who made a study of the Shuswap. Their studies were published in 1909, the year I was born. Long after I had written *The Double Hook* I became interested in the work of an anthropologist called Wilson Duff. Phyllis Webb's most recent book, *Wilson's Bowl*, refers to Duff, who studied the stone sculptures of the West Coast Indians and insisted in a Poundian way that the images were not just visual but that they embodied a kind of mathematical logic, as Levi-Strauss might argue.

Interviewers: Your work contains mythopoeic elements without any slavish reiteration of them.

Watson: That's not unusual of course. For instance when I was reading Zola I realized how much of his work is patterned on mythic structures although he was an acclaimed naturalist. I think he used the myths purposely as structural devices. You find the same thing in a novel like Flaubert's *Sentimental Education* where underneath the whole political thing is the primitive cave in Chartres which was the temple of the mother goddess on which Chartres was built.

Interviewers: Is it possible to say, as Robert Graves does, that there is one story and one story only?

Watson: I'm not sure. I don't like reductive theories—like the theory that poems are made out of other poems. In one sense they are but not in any literal sense. No mind is innocent. By the time I wrote *The Double Hook*, for instance, I had read Yeats, Eliot, Joyce, Pound. Their work had left its traces, become part of my thinking.

Interviewers: Many of your characters seem obsessive and these obsessions seem to function for them as a way of shutting themselves off from the world.

Watson: I think perhaps that is true—certainly Uncle Daedalus in one of the short stories is—and Oedipus in another. One should fear obsession.

Interviewers: You have said that literature is not innocent.

Watson: I don't think words are innocent. Sometimes the impact of words on a reader is not what the writer expects at all. In that sense they are not innocent. The reader has a creative function which the words provoke. Words are not simple exchange. They are charged. They have all sorts of possibilities which may explode at any moment. There are moments, for instance, when one is reading poetry aloud when one senses that one can't go on because the listeners can't bear it. Sometimes, too, there are books that one simply cannot read because they are too powerful, too disturbing. I remember an incident connected with Elias Canetti's *Auto da Fé*. It is a terrifying book. I gave it to someone who simply couldn't read it. That, I suppose, is what I mean when I say literature is not innocent because it has the power to produce a disequilibrium in your life. Or, as Marshall McLuhan would say, it is a kind of transgression.

Interviewers: A violation?

Watson: Yes, a violation, a transgression of sensibility. It is not a pacifier.

Interviewers: Is it something inherent in the very nature of language?

Watson: Yes. As Ricoeur said, man is freed from his animal condition but he is freed into a more perilous condition through language. I've always felt that.

Interviewers: Are there any innocent characters in your works?

Watson: (Pause.) No.

Interviewers: Has your husband, the poet Wilfred Watson, been an influence on your work?

Watson: Any mind with which you are seriously in contact is an influence.

Interviewers: Are there certain works and authors you tend to return to?

Watson: I have often reread Dostoyevsky's *The Possessed*, not *The Brothers Karamazov*, and recently I reread Gogol's *The Overcoat* and his *Dead Souls*, probably because I read them when I was quite young like other people of my age—and as the Australian poet Alec Hope reminded me, in bad translations. I don't particularly like having to reread Virginia Woolf or the writers associated with her. I thought they had a soft focus which seemed sentimental. I read and reread more poetry than fiction.

Interviewers: You had an early interest in Swift?

Watson: Oh yes and I reread Swift. I also had an interest in Wyndham Lewis. I was attracted to both of them because I am interested in satire. Recently I reread Faulkner...

Interviewers: There's an interesting parallel between your work and Faulkner's in the emphasis which you place on the family unit. Is it possible to say that the tensions of the family unit form the basis of your myth?

Watson: The family as exclusive unit? That's Greta's problem in *The Double Hook*. She needs something to love and she loves James because there is no one else there. It is a displaced love. The emphasis in *The Double Hook* is not on family but on the problem of a community reduced almost to a single unit. The sequence of events in town show just how narrow that community is.

Interviewers: You almost seem to be saying at the end of the novel that the characters may have achieved a certain kind of freedom but that it would be unwise to believe that they have, therefore, freed the next generation, because the next generation is also going to have to struggle.

Watson: Yes, and for the same reason.

Interviewers: There is a theatrical, cinematic form to the novel. Have there been any attempts to film it?

Watson: A former student of mine, Sam Koplowicz, began to work on it as his film thesis at Stanford. He, and eventually a friend of his, Bill Pasnak, wrote several scripts but they had a great deal of difficulty with it because even if it seems to be written in a cinematic fashion it really isn't. The images are not really visual images although they may seem photographic. The novel depends on its verbal structure. They had serious trouble with the scripting. Koplowicz worked for a long time on the project. He even found locations in the Cariboo and a house to burn. Had they managed to film it, it would have been their thing. They were completely involved. Otherwise I was never anxious to see it filmed because I've seen too many novels ruined on film. You can't always translate from one medium to another. *The Double Hook* was written to be read.

Interviewers: You followed *The Double Hook*, not with another novel, but with a collection of short stories.

Watson: Yes. They were written about the same time as *The Double Hook*. Three of them were published before *The Double Hook*. "The Rumble Seat" was written much later. It began as a satire on Pierre Berton's *The Comfortable Pew*.

Interviewers: We were very struck by the story "Antigone". It seems to contain autobiographical elements.

Watson: Yes, you are right in terms of place. I was brought up in the Provincial Mental Hospital in British Columbia on the banks of the Fraser River in New Westminster. I don't know whether you have seen the dust jacket on the Coach House Press collection. They were going to put a black barn on the cover but I found an old bronze tint of the mental hospital taken about the time I was born, with the gardener I remembered raking the garden. The Press took it and put some colour in it and that's the dust jacket of the book. I was, virtually, born in the mental hospital and lived there for the first eleven years of my life. My father was the Superintendent, the doctor in charge. We lived right in the institution, in an apartment. That autobiographical fact underlies "Antigone". I didn't want to write about a mental hospital per se. I wanted to raise an essential question—what is madness?

Interviewers: It must have been an unusual childhood for you, then, in that you must have realized that you could walk out of there any time whereas the patients could not.

Watson: Well, no, that wasn't quite the case. We lived in a very disciplined environment. We had our own keeper, too, a Scots Presbyterian nanny. My father had, for the time, some fairly unusual ideas about the treatment of mental illness. For instance, when he first took over he destroyed all the box beds and straight jackets and took all the guards off the gates and he created an experimental farm. The purpose of this was to bring the patients out of themselves. The farm was both therapeutic and was also innovative in terms of agricultural experiments that were carried on there. The whole point was to make everything more human. The atmosphere of the place had a great influence on me. We were never allowed to call the place 'the asylum', although people did. We were taught to call it the hospital. It was technically known as Number 9, in the way the Queen Street Mental Hospital here used to be referred to as Number 999.

Interviewers: Where did you draw the line between your world and that of the patients?

Watson: You didn't draw a line. I accepted where I was because it seemed the most natural thing in the world. Perhaps that is why I often think of the world as a sort of institution. In an autobiographical sense anything I have written about childhood is grounded in that experience. About what else could I write directly? We lived in a very clinical enclosed world. I suppose the father figure in "Antigone" is my own father. I remember when I was small we had a pony which one of the patients named Jack looked after. I remember my father calling me into his office and saying, "What did you say to Jack?" And I must have had a bad conscience about it and admitted that I had said " 'You're crazy, Jack,' but I meant it just in a general sense, without thinking." And my father just looked at me and said, "It's not what you mean, it's what you say." I can still hear him now. It is not what you mean, it is what you say. That was probably the most fundamental single influence on my attitude to language.

Interviewers: How do you feel about how people have reacted to what you say as opposed to what you mean?

Watson: You can't control response. I am unhappy when people describe *The Double Hook* as a prose poem because that phrase makes me think of purple passages and things like that. It has been said that technically it is not a novel and perhaps it isn't. It is a narrative structure of some kind.

Interviewers: Have you written much poetry?

Watson: I wrote one poem which was published in *The Canadian Forum* but I didn't write poetry after that. What appear to be poems in *The Double Hook* are actually, in many instances, the echo of Biblical passages which act like the choruses in the Greek dramas.

Interviewers: Turning to your short stories, were there particular technical difficulties with the form that you chose?

Watson: The difficulty was practical. If it hadn't been for Malcom Ross, who was editing *The Queen's Quarterly*, probably they would never have been published. Just as, if it hadn't been for Jack McClelland *The Double Hook* wouldn't have been published. He accepted it as it stood and tried to deal with it. He published books which would not have been considered commercially viable at the time. He took risks when he believed in something. He reassured me about *The Double Hook*. He said, "It may not sell well at first but it will eventually repay my publication costs." And I imagine it has.

Interviewers: The jacket of the first edition of the book has a hook on it. What is the background?

Watson: The background in the cover designed by Frank Newfeld is a photograph of the cross section of a tibia bone. It is a very interesting cover. It was a sensitive and creative response to the text. The cover on the most recent printing of the paperback edition is another matter. It is a photograph from the Glenbow Museum of a woman pumping water. She is surrounded by cows and chickens. I suppose it is meant to be Greta. If it was intended to suggest that the novel is regional it failed to identify the specific region. It was a cliché in both senses of the word—a photograph of a pioneer prairie wife. It saddened me because I had tried to avoid the trap of regionalism as that term is understood. In designing the original cover Frank Newfeld had drawn attention to the title not to my name. He knew I wanted to disappear from the book. The paperback reverses the emphasis.

Interviewers: You have avoided a larger-than-life public persona. Is that a conscious strategy?

Watson: I've wanted what is on the page to speak for itself. I've never, not even now, wanted to talk about what I have written, which—after all—is a very small body of work.

Brian Moore
In Celebration of the Commonplace

After having given a speech in Toronto for the city's part in the celebration of the James Joyce Centenary, the Irish-Canadian writer, Brian Moore, consented to an interview. "Do you mind us taping it?" Moore replied: "Just as long as you clean up my language. After all, I'm a novelist and an Irishman."

Born in Belfast in 1921, Moore came to Canada in 1948 and worked as a journalist in Montreal before embarking on a career as a novelist and sometime screenwriter. He currently lives in California, but has retained his Canadian citizenship. In 1960 he won the Governor-General's Award for his novel *The Luck of Ginger Coffey*. Moore has an international audience of readers which includes fans such as Graham Greene and film director John Huston.

Interviewers: We live in an age where often there is more attention paid to a writer's life than is paid to his work. Has this been a problem for you?

Moore: There are people now reading biographies of W.H. Auden and Robert Lowell, who probably have read very little of their work. And then you have the examples of Mailer, Capote and Vidal, whose lives are of more interest to people than their work. So, in the case of a writer like myself, who has simply a private life and not a very colourful legend, the only things people can fasten onto are details like my nationality. I think it is irrelevant myself because with a writer it is what he writes that is of interest and not his life. If in my book I seem to be an Irish writer, then the reader thinks he's in the presence of an Irish writer. If he thinks I'm a Canadian, then he thinks he's in the presence of a Canadian writer. I think nationality is something Canadians worry about unduly. A good example is Nabokov, who at one time was a White Russian, then had British citizenship, and then became an American citizen. Then he left America when he had made enough money and went to live in Montreuil for the rest of his life. But the Americans always accepted him as an American author. In all the years I've lived in America, there's always been this question of whether or not I'm a Canadian author. Overall, though, I'm a writer who has no personal grievances because for the past twenty-five years I've been able to write what I wanted to write, and that makes me one of the lucky few.

Interviewers: Graham Greene has called you his favourite living writer. Do you return the compliment?

Moore: Well, I've wondered if it is often the case that writers you like also like you. I admire Graham Greene's work and I've learned a lot from him. Greene and Waugh are the two pre-eminent English writers of their generation. They are pre-eminent in prose just as Larkin is in poetry. People that like Greene usually like Waugh. And people who like Waugh and Greene usually like Larkin. One tends to like writers in which one sees something of oneself. I'm very lucky that Graham Greene said that about me because it has helped my sales enormously. For instance, in faraway countries where they've never heard of anyone other than Graham Greene, his reference to me has been particularly useful. In one South American edition of *The Doctor's Wife*, Greene's quotation about me was used and it helped sell thirty-seven thousand copies. If I sold that many in the United States of a hardcover edition, I'd be very lucky.

Interviewers: Have you ever met Greene?

Moore: I met him once years ago in Montreal. It was only very briefly. I had only just finished my first novel and was introduced to him by the editor of *The Montreal Star* and we went out on the town together for the evening. I met him on one other occasion in Montreal when he passed through, but I can't really say that I know him.

Interviewers: Many of your novels don't deal directly with politics per se, except in the case of *The Revolution Script*. In this sense you are also like Greene.

Moore: Well, I started as a newspaperman and I learned from that that novelists can't possibly keep up with all the news and information today. For instance, if you set out to write a novel today about El Salvador, by the time it was published nine months later, it would probably be out-of-date. So I fear political subjects are very ephemeral. They are not a great subject for a novel today unless you have an exceptional experience like Solzhenitsyn. But to go and report on things journalistically, as novelists did in the nineteenth century, is a waste of time. Other media will cover these things much more accurately. Also, it is interesting that a political situation such as that in Northern Ireland has really not been touched directly by any major writer. Seamus Heaney doesn't write directly about it and neither does anyone else. My feeling about novels is that people are born, married, they fight and they die and various things happen to everyone—these are the subjects which interest me more rather than whether they were born on the right or wrong side of privilege.

Interviewers: Nevertheless, you did tackle a political subject in *The Revolution Script.*

Moore: That was a mistake. I wanted to do a non-fiction book and I started to do it out of a belief that Trudeau, in invoking the War Measures Act, was acting in the same way as the British had in Northern Ireland for twenty years. He was repressing liberty. And I saw too that the anglophone liberal people here were completely blind to that because they were afraid of the French. When I started to write the book I was trapped by the fact that I couldn't make direct contact with the terrorists. When the terrorists were allowed to flee to Cuba in the middle of my book, I had to make them fictional characters. I knew they weren't going to come back and sue me. (Laughter.) The book was an experiment but I don't regard it as part of my work but rather as some journalistic exercise.

Interviewers: You seem to write a great deal about the loss of faith in the face of personal adversity. You suggest that it is very important for one to develop some system of personal moral values, in order to stay sane, to have some constants and anchors in one's life. For instance, Judith Hearne has pictures of her aunt and the Sacred Heart and Ginger Coffey has his family. In traditional literature it is the artist, the intellectual, the aristocrat who has come to terms with the problems of faith in himself and in others. You seem to be more interested in the ordinary person's loss of faith. Do you see that as the common theme in your work?

Moore: There are certain continuing preoccupations in my novels, but, yes, I decided very early on that Joyce had written about an intellectual's loss of faith in *A Portrait of the Artist as a Young Man*, and I decided I couldn't compete with that. I also recognized, however, that Joyce himself, my great hero, had said that his work was a celebration of the common-place, and I feel that my writing is also a celebration of the commonplace. I believe that the most interesting lives are the

lives of ordinary people. Most of us can't relate to someone
who is extraordinarily intelligent or extraordinarily dumb
because most of us fall somewhere in between. I am interested
in the point in ordinary people's lives when, like all of us,
there's a carrot held out in front of them—like ambition. My
novels often revolve around the moment in that person's life
when to remove that carrot of ambition or desire, the person
is forced, within a certain period of time, to re-evaluate their
lives and make a decision about what they are going to do.
I'm interested in the moment in which one's illusions are
shattered and one has to live without *the* faith, whatever that
faith was which originally sustained them. I also like in novels
to start the clock ticking. I like the novel to take place within a
certain time. I have to explain to the reader what made this
particular time different. That to me is the natural moment of
fiction, the natural moment of crisis. I do this in order to inject
an element of suspense. I've come to have a greater interest in
the element of suspense as I grow older. For instance, I will
now look at Conrad's *The Secret Agent* in a way I would not
when I was young. I look at the suspense in Graham Greene
or Borges in a way which didn't interest me when I was
younger. My new book, *Cold Heaven*, is a curious book in that
for the first one hundred and fifty pages you believe you are
reading a thriller because you don't know what's happening
to the character. It moves very quickly, but on a rather
mundane level, the way thrillers do, and then you discover,
halfway through the book, that this isn't an ordinary
thriller—it is a metaphysical thriller, about something more
mysterious than that contained in an ordinary thriller. I don't
think I would have written a book that way ten years ago.
This is a culmination of my experiments along the same lines
in *The Temptation of Eileen Hughes* and *The Mangan Inheritance*.
Cold Heaven goes one step further. So, willy-nilly, I'm going
through a cycle of books in the suspense genre. It is important
to realize that what I'm trying to do is not write books that are
detective stories, but rather are novels of suspense in the
detective mode. The power of withholding information from

the reader, but not dishonestly, the power of narrative, of unfolding a story by turning pages, builds narrative suspense, which is interesting for your writing because it forces you to write more leanly—in a direct, clear, clean way. My style has been evolving towards a more plain style. Reviewers have said that when I use a simile or metaphor it stands out. It is not simply piling on description. When I do finally say something about a character, it hits, it has a very big power. I think that is something which is the result of this very visual age we live in. People can't read in the way they used to because their mind's eye is making cinematic cuts. We see prose passages now as films because children are brought up looking at film all the time. I've always thought that the modern reader made jump-cuts just like directors in films. I think we could move fiction into the realm of short-takes, a way which has not really been attempted. Someday, someone will come up with a type of fiction which approximates the cinematic, and that will have a very interesting effect.

Interviewers: What about Kosinski and Robbe-Grillet?

Moore: There's no movement in Robbe-Grillet. He just pans around and looks at furniture, and as for Kosinski, he's just a bad writer, so I'm not the person to really discuss him. Whereas, if you take an older writer like Evelyn Waugh, he can take two men in a room and you can *see* exactly what they are doing, but in very understated prose. Similarly, Greene is one of the great scene-setters of all time. Their techniques are very cinematic. We tend to take cinematic as a pejorative word in writing, but I'm not using it that way at all.

Interviewers: You seem to be saying that the novel has a future.

Moore: I don't have any theories about "the novel". I find that experimental writing, unless it is truly experimental, is one of the most easily fakeable things in the world. One of the most truly experimental writers in the world is Flann O'Brien. The writing goes beyond Joyce into something that is absolutely brilliant. Borges is a truly experimental writer, also

Gabriel Garcia Marquez. John Barth isn't. With these academic writers, it's all just Twenties' hokum revamped and regurgitated. It is unreadable and it is junk. I think most writers in their heart of hearts suspect that it is junk.

Interviewers: So when someone sits down to read a book of yours...

Moore: I want them to read for pleasure, I want to move people. I find that unless I'm going to do better than *Ulysses*, I don't want to write an experimental novel. Although, I am among Joyce's greatest admirers, I think *Finnegans Wake* is a great mistake. No one reads *Finnegans Wake* for pleasure, nor have they ever. The suspicious thing about most of this so-called experimental writing is that it is instantly teachable. The old, bad schlock writers like Irving Wallace and Robert Ludlum—all these people like the old storytellers, write in a very bad way, a very cliched way, but they write within a very strong framework of narrative, a strong framework of dream. Their books are wet dreams for college-educated people. They have that power. They are the obverse to me of the Barthian academic novelist, who is equally cliched and equally bored. I suffer from two things that prevent me from having a big audience. One is that I'm a nomad, and, two, I don't write the same book over and over again. There isn't a continuity to my books where people can say: "That's a Brian Moore". I have a continuing set of preoccupations, but I experiment with form. It is like what Greene said about me, I'm like a lion-tamer with the novel. It hasn't been a conscious strategy of mine to avoid being labelled English-Canadian or Irish-American because I would like to be claimed by everybody, and to have a readership in each of these places. I didn't have an Irish readership for a very long time because the clergy had my books banned in Ireland. Irish people thought for a long time that I was an American or a Canadian. The only good piece of luck I've had in this matter is that since my first book was published in England, the English always treated each book as a book by itself. So right from the very beginning in England, I've always had respectful, good reviews of my work. They are the only people who have never mentioned my nationality.

Interviewers: You mentioned that there were certain continuing preoccupations in your novels. Could you talk about some of them?

Moore: I suppose unlike most male novelists today, Catholicism continues to be something that I write about. I'm interested in the church as an organism. I'm interested in loneliness. I've always considered myself one of life's rejects. I came from a family of successful people—my father was a great achiever in examinations and things like that. I failed my examinations at school. I was very bad at math which in those days was the end—if you couldn't get math you couldn't get anything. I could never become a doctor because I was not good at chemistry. I was thirty before I wrote my first novel so I had quite a bit of experience at being a failure before I became a quasi-success.

Interviewers: Your novels tend to contain a rather bleak vision...

Moore: I think that's true. I tend to try to examine the dichotomy between what people think they are and what they do. A wonderful book could be written about Hitler's image of Hitler. Hitler didn't see himself as he was and neither did Attila the Hun. It is interesting that monsters don't know they are monsters and to my mind everyone has a totally false notion of their own worth. Some people are modest to the point of not realizing their true worth, but they are a small minority.

Interviewers: Did you ever have a mentor or a particular teacher who influenced you or encouraged you when you were young?

Moore: Yes. When I was seven or eight, I remember the headmaster calling me in, and asking me to fill a notebook with essays on topics like what I did on my summer vacation. I was very flattered and happy to take the week off from studies to write for him. I wrote seven or eight essays and he used those essays for three or four years after. So, I was given this inflated notion of myself when I was very small. I wasn't as successful in any of my other subjects, so I got this notion of myself as a writer, but I was intimidated by other writers that I read and thought I could never equal them. So, I thought the next best thing I could do was to become a newspaper reporter. It was only after I had read a couple of bad books written by people that I knew that I decided I could do better than that. I thought that poor books were more important to read than Tolstoy.

Interviewers: Like Brendan Tierney in *An Answer from Limbo?*

Moore: Yes. I use that example. I seem to be at variance with most modern writers. When you read interviews with them they seem to say that writing is torture, that it is hell and how when they go through it they sweat blood and this sort of thing. I find that writing is torture. It is hell to get it right, but I'm only happy when I am writing. Why I write so much is that I'm happy when I am writing, not when I'm teaching or being interviewed. (Laughter.) I can live quite a solitary, monkish life because I'm not intimidated by the act of getting up in the morning and continuing to write a novel. I suppose that there are more writers like me, but they feel that is is impolitic to admit it.

Interviewers: When you were writing *The Mangan Inheritance* you had a very severe illness, and you've said that the act of writing helped you to pull out of it. Has writing become something a little more special for you since then?

Moore: I discovered during that period that I was too tired and too ill to read but I was able to write. So it had an influence. I was very close to death for quite a long time. That focussed my attention very closely on the years that I have left. Until I had the illness, I felt life was a perpetual party. After the illness I became aware that it might not be.

Interviewers: Also during the composition of *The Mangan Inheritance* you switched genres from a novel of manners to a gothic horror. This was quite a gamble. Do you see yourself as a literary risk-taker?

Moore: I do, indeed. For many reviewers and readers *The Mangan Inheritance* was too big a gamble. If I had a commercial mind, I would have written *The Mangan Inheritance* as a gothic horror and the book would have opened in Ireland. I would have had an enormously successful book because the whole Irish section is written in a more elevated, charismatic way, and the characters seem more interesting. The Canadian-American part of that book is written on a realistic level. One editor in fact suggested to me that I put the Canadian-American past in simply as a flash-back. But I felt, as I always feel, that that would be a deception for the reader. The interest in *The Mangan Inheritance* should be that this is a person like you or me who is projected into this milieu. He should act as you or I would in a similar predicament. I knew I was taking risks, but I also knew that I would be cheating if I did it any other way.

Interviewers: How does a novel start for you?

Moore: I start with a character and keep changing my opinion of him. By starting that way I feel I get to know him or her. It is like when you first meet a stranger. You have some fixed ideas about what they are like and gradually you get to know them and trust them. In my writing you trust to the instinct of the character which makes you know not to make them do something outré because they just wouldn't do that. That defines your plot. I hate killing people in a novel because you don't go around indiscriminately killing people in real life. Death in a novel should be as momentous as it is in real life.

Interviewers: You've never written a novel that was entirely a flashback, but you have indicated that you once thought of writing a screen-play for *Judith Hearne*, which would have been almost entirely in flashback. Do you think in retrospect that the novel would have worked better as a flashback or did you simply think that, in cinematic terms, it would have worked better as a flashback?

Moore: I must have been desperately trying to find some way to answer an interviewer's question. (Laughter.) I've talked to students about flashbacks in that way. Quite often when young writers start a story they start with a scene and the scene may last for two and a half pages, and then they decide I've got to tell the reader all about this person and they go into a flashback which lasts five and a half pages. I say to them, flashbacks should be small digressions. I have very strong feelings that you should never have a whole chapter in flashback because it can become another book. Either the narrative must keep moving forward and can't be interrupted or else the digression must neatly fit into the narrative. You can't be back-peddling. If you keep flashing back, then why should you go on?

Interviewers: Flashbacks take away from the element of building up suspense.

Moore: Yes, they do. You're damaging the narrative in that sense. The flashback is also a convention that was much more prevalent twenty years ago.

Interviewers: In both journalism and the cinema, one to a large extent is forced to shape the narrative in the present tense. Has your background as a journalist and as a screenwriter for John Huston and Alfred Hitchcock influenced you to write primarily in the present tense?

Moore: Yes, insofar as in the newspaper business you are concerned with the same questions that concern the novelist —who, what, when, why, where. Also, as a journalist, you get a microcosm of what is going on in society. You have to deal with present-day events—which bank was robbed today, that sort of thing.

Interviewers: How did you come to work with Alfred Hitchcock?

Moore: Alfred Hitchcock read my book, *The Feast of Lupercal*, and liked it. He had also gone to a Jesuit school and so identified with the setting of the novel. As a result of reading that book, he hired me to do the screenplay for *Torn Curtain* with Paul Newman and Julie Andrews.

Interviewers: How did you and Hitchcock get along?

Moore: The problem I had with Hitchcock was that he was a living legend. He'd done fifty films and I'd done zero, so I tended to take his word for everything. When we finished doing the script I thought it was very bad. I felt the characters were cardbaord, and I made the mistake of telling him that. He was never a person who would have a confrontation with you to your face. He just simply hired two other screen-writers, and they were not able to change it. So I wound up getting sole credit for the script, which I'm not very proud of. I don't think I'm a Hitchcockian writer. I think by the time I met him he believed his own legend. It was hard to explain to him that these characters didn't seem real to me, that I didn't think it was going to work. One of the problems was that it was one of the most expensive films that Hitchcock ever made.

Interviewers: How about John Huston? He was also a legend by the time you met him.

Moore: Well, Huston was totally different. He is one of the few really brilliant people I've ever dealt with. He came to see me about my novel, *Catholics*, and suggested that I turn it into a film. He said, "It should only take you two or three weeks". Well, it almost killed me. These things take longer than that. He then called me and said that it would make a good television film, rather than a feature film. I thought, then, that he was kind of brushing me off, but actually he wasn't. He said he would direct it, but unfortunately the television network didn't see it that way because they felt he would be too expensive. He would have been a very interesting director to work with. You know he bought *Judith Hearne* at one point.

Interviewers: Katherine Hepburn was supposed to star in it wasn't she?

Moore: The studios didn't want her for the part. I had no say, of course, in that decision. This is one of the objections I have to working in film. The writer just has to do what he is told to do. I mean, the problem is that there is so much money involved. It is as if when you are writing a book you are told from the outset that this must sell 250,000 copies in paperback and be a Book-of-the-Month Club selection and be translated into eighteen foreign languages, or else it is a failure. There are too many masters to please in film. There's a confusion in people's minds today between art and commerce, which I think has made for a situation where even serious books are a risky business as compared to twenty-five years ago. When I first started being published it didn't cost very much for a novel to be published. You could live comfortably on five-thousand dollars a year. If you sold enough to cover the costs of a small paperback edition then everybody was happy, and you could go on to the next book. I think it is very sad for the young writer today who has a first novel. He has to be an instant success so he doesn't really have time to develop as a writer.

Interviewers: Do you think the novel will go the way of poetry, in terms of substantially decreased sales and influence?

Moore: I would hate to think that. Part of the confusion is in our own minds. We do tend to equate, certainly the Americans do, literary with commercial success, even at the highest level. Can you think of a Canadian writer who is more highly regarded even though he has smaller sales than any of those who have the large sales? We tend to think of the successful writer as the one who sells a lot.

Interviewers: Did you ever write poetry?

Moore: No, not really. I would love to have had it in me.

Interviewers: Which Canadian writers do you read yourself?

Moore: I've read quite a lot of them. I think my favourite Canadian writer at the moment is Alice Munro. Once again, I like those people whose writing has some affinity with my own. Alice Munro, for me, captures a sense of Canada. I like Richard Wright. None of the writers I like are what I would call academics.

Interviewers: Can you tell us what you're working on now?

Moore: I've had to write five hours worth of a television script based on a book by Simone de Beauvoir and I had to invent new characters. I know the period and I know France well, so I had an advantage in that. The people who hired me were very enlightened, compared to the average movie people, in that they left me alone to work on it. I didn't have to attend a lot of meetings about it and I was able to get it done in time—in four months.

Interviewers: Are you ruthless with your time?

Moore: Yes, I have to be. I did meet with them yesterday and they agreed with my judgement that we had to cut it down by an hour. So that's what I'm doing now.

Interviewers: How did you feel about working with someone else's novel?

Moore: It is easier than working with your own, because you have already seen your novel as a novel. Someone else's work you can approach just as a story—this one is a love story, a period story about Vichy and the Jews.

Interviewers: One other thing we've noticed about your work, there are very few overt, literary references.

Moore: Yes, well I don't think of my work in Ph.D. thesis terms. I've always felt that if you can illuminate a particular situation, absolutely and truly, and if the situation is intrinsically of interest, that will become the archetypal situation. The mistake made in so much bad fiction is to try to take an archetypal situation and then try to get a character to fit the thesis of the novel—the novel written around a thesis. For instance, a writer decides, "I am going to write a novel about infidelity or about the loss of God". Well, my own approach would be: "What if so-and-so lost their faith? What would they think? How would they behave? What would they do?" I didn't realize it, but in *Judith Hearne* I was writing about the loss of faith, about the loss of faith in one ordinary person. But what I did without knowing it was write an archetypal model of a novel about lonely women. Of all my books it is the one that has stayed in print most constantly. It touched some very raw, sensitive nerve among women and especially among lonely women, or women who feared they would be lonely. It has outlived feminism and every faddish shade of opinion about women. If I had planned that the book should have this effect, it would be dead and forgotten—as would all my books.

Elizabeth Smart

Fact and Emotional Truth

The cicadas were buzzing in the maple trees of downtown Toronto's Annex district on the day we arrived to interview Elizabeth Smart. She greeted us at the top of a long winding flight of worn, pale-cream stairs. She showed us out to a metal balcony at the side of the building. Through the metal slats of the balcony the leaves of what appeared to be a giant sumach poked through at our feet.

Interviewers: These are very tall sumachs.

Smart: But they aren't sumachs. They're 'trees of heaven'.

Interviewers: Trees of heaven? There's a lot of metaphorical mileage to be got out of that.

Smart: I love them. They're called trees of heaven because they were once planted by the Chinese Emperors in the gardens of the Heavenly Palace in Peking. They grow so tall and look like ladders. They've made it up this far at least. Let's go inside.

She showed us into a white, neatly-kept room where she lounged on a day-bed in the corner. The windows, shaded by the tops of maples, were open as thunder rolled in the distance.

Born in 1913 to a wealthy Ottawa family, she was educated at private schools and through a series of "grand tours" to Europe and the British Isles, before embarking on a life that included one of the most discussed literary and emotional relationships of this century, her love affair with British poet George Barker. The events and effects of this liaison formed the basis for her first published novel, *By Grand Central Station I Sat Down and Wept* (1945), which since its recent reissue in paperback has enjoyed a cult following. This success was followed after more than twenty years with a second novel, *The Assumption of the Rogues and Rascals* (1978), and two volumes of verse, *A Bonus* (1977) and *Eleven Poems* (1982). When we talked to her she had recently completed the 1982-83 academic year as Writer-in-Residence at the University of Alberta in Edmonton, a position for which she was recommended by poet Pat Lane.

Interviewers: Could you talk about what you are working on now?

Smart: No. That's one question I can't answer. First, there's the superstition about it all. The minute you say it or talk about it, it all slips away. When I went out to the University of Alberta as Writer-in-Residence one thing I had to do to justify my salary was to write a prospectus of my current and future work. I was very excited about a project I had in mind, but as soon as I wrote about it, it went out like a light—it was just flat. All the other writers I've talked to will never tell each other what they're working on. You can't easily talk it out. When you conceive something like a novel you have the pressure there to create it, but when you talk about it, the pressure to create somehow dissipates.

Interviewers: Do you think the character of your writing has changed since the early days when you wrote *By Grand Central Station I Sat Down and Wept?*

Smart: I don't think it has essentially, but I do hope it has improved. Perhaps it has gotten a bit bonier. My verses are very bony. My prose is rather well-upholstered I'd say, but I think it is getting more so—I can't keep off the metaphors and so forth. One always hopes one's improving, learning something.

Interviewers: When did you first start writing?

Smart: Very young. When I was about ten.

Interviewers: What made you start writing?

Smart: First, there was this silly poem. A teacher at school liked it. She was one of those people who inspire you, and I sent it off to an American magazine for children and it was accepted and printed and I got a dollar for it. And then I got inspirations where I'd sit and write quite a few at a time. I produced a whole volume.

Interviewers: But it was never published.

Smart: No, but it resides now in the National Library. It was called *The Second Edition of the Complete Works of B. Smart.*

Interviewers: What were some of the early influences on you?

Smart: Ernest Thompson Seton, the animal writer, and J.M. Barrie who wrote *Peter Pan.*

Interviewers: When you say Seton, what was it about him? Was he simply your current reading at the time?

Smart: I loved animals. I was mad about animals to the exclusion of everything else until I was about eleven. I wouldn't read anything else. Then I was in bed for a year and somebody brought me J.M. Barrie and I got some ideas about style. We used to have compulsory readings of Dickens which I thought I hated but now when I look back on writers such as Dickens I see that they were valuable. I was so ill during this period that I wasn't allowed out of bed to get up to go to the bathroom. The doctor claimed I had a leaking valve in my heart. After all that time in bed I had to learn to walk again. Because of that I've always felt very close to the little mermaid of Hans Christian Andersen's story. Every step was painful because my feet hadn't touched the floor so long.

Interviewers: Was there one particular event that triggered your early rebellion?

Smart: I don't really think I've been all that rebellious. I don't hold with that idea. I was always trying to conform as much as I could. I went to Elmwood School where everyone was English and they were trying to civilize the natives—very snobby. I, however, had a very strong feeling for being Canadian. I guess I was rebellious in terms of the fact that I wanted to sever Canada from the mother country. That was my political time. (Laughter.) In nature study, for example, we learned all the British birds—the difference, for instance, between a rook and a crow. Well, there aren't any rooks in Canada. Of course, we weren't taught anything about Canadian history. I was twelve at the time. They tried to give us English accents but that made us even more Canadian! My family had been on this continent for several generations, originally from New England. They were Pennyslvania Dutch and French Huguenot on my mother's side and Sioux Indian which I'm still very proud of. So there was no English in us at all you see. We were part Scottish and Irish at a later point. They came up from New England for the lumber in 1855.

Interviewers: You mother discouraged you from attending university.

Smart: Yes. Back in those days it was considered unlady-like to pass your matriculation.

Interviewers: But not to travel. Is it true you went on twenty-two trans-Atlantic trips during your teens?

Smart: Oh yes. That's quite accurate. And it was lovely. It used to take eleven days unless you got one of the very fast boats. The ship was its own little world. I wrote it all down, you know. I never stopped writing up until the time that I started having children.

Interviewers: What influence did those early travels have on you?

Smart: As a novelist it was interesting because you met such a variety of people and had the chance to study them. I've always loved funny characters, odd people and the things they do. At my parents' home, people were always dropping in on Sundays for a visit—I called them the "odds and ends." They used to be wonderful days. We'd go swimming and then we'd come back and my mother always prepared a marvellous meal and the "odds and ends" didn't need much encouragement to stay on. I wrote about them in a lot of my early stories.

Interviewers: You were encouraged quite early on by Lawrence Durrell.

Smart: Yes. When I first got to London I sent out poems to all the little magazines. Durrell was editing one called *Blast*—no, pardon me, that was Pound's—Durrell ran one called *Boost* which lasted only one issue. He was going to publish my poem in the second. But he wrote me a nice letter and asked what Canada was like and we struck up a correspondence. He encouraged me quite a bit when he wasn't asking questions about Mazo de la Roche.

Interviewers: You've written several unpublished novels, such as *Let Us Dig a Grave and Bury Our Mother.*

Smart: That was the book I wrote before *By Grand Central.* Those early novels were just really exercises. I don't think they're good enough to be published. I really would like to publish *Let Us Dig a Grave* because I almost incorporated it into the new thing I was planning when I was out West. But I just think it is not quite good enough.

Interviewers: What was it about?

Smart: It was about one's relationship with one's mother. It was about a woman who has a relationship with another woman which eventually reconciles the character to her mother. *Let Us Dig a Grave* had lots of characters in it.

Interviewers: What finally made you decide to write *By Grand Central Station I Sat Down and Wept?*

Smart: I don't think I really decided to write it. You don't really decide these things.

Interviewers: So the early novel, *Let Us Dig a Grave*, was just a training novel.

Smart: And so was the one before that, *My Lover John*, which was about male impotence. Neither novel was very bad, but they couldn't be published now. They're just not good enough.

Interviewers: Was there any particular event that triggered the writing of *By Grand Central?*

Smart: Not really. I was just thinking of this particular subject—you might call it passionate love or something. I fell in love and that happens to most people. I just happened to be writing at the time.

Interviewers: The border incident section in *By Grand Central* is one that you frequently read at public readings.

Smart: Yes, it was one of the last sections written for the book. I get confused myself now because people are apt to tell you what you did. The beginning of the last section was one of the first parts I wrote. The opening section of the novel was written second. The whole work was written in sections, but I realized I needed more to connect it all together so I wrote about the border incident. I like to read that particular section at readings because it takes exactly seven and a half minutes to get through—long enough to be interesting and short enough not to lose anyone's attention. So you see I'm very practical about these things. In fact, you'd be amazed at how practical my life really is.

Interviewers: How did you hit upon the very unique structure that you used in *By Grand Central?*

Smart: By luck if it is successful, by ill-luck if it is unsuccessful. I did study music and as you'll notice there are movements to the novel just as there are in symphonies. A point-counterpoint. I don't know of much music that's in ten parts like my novel.

Interviewers: You've said that by now you aren't sure what are the actual events and what are the fictional events in the novel. Where does one draw the line between fiction and actuality? Is it memory which blurs that distinction?

Smart: George Barker and I were talking about this, recently, at the Edinburgh Festival—about the difference between fact and emotional truth. The two things are quite different. Something might be factually untrue but might be emotionally true. Therefore, it is fiction and it is made with what one hopes is art. If you have emotion but you have no craft, then you will not have art. You have to have the craft first otherwise there's no point in having any emotions. You can gather a million facts but what's the point of it?

Interviewers: So, it is the balance, then, between emotion, craft and fact that makes fiction?

Smart: Yes. You have to use your craft to render accurately the emotional feeling. I think the hardest emotion to render is anger because anger is gone so quickly. When you feel it you are absolutely in a rage and you could murder for that minute but someone comes in the door and you make it into a funny story immediately. I've never really managed to convey anger. I'm always afraid of turning it into diatribe, but perhaps someday I'll manage to write it. Even in real life I'll just splutter a cry if I get really angry.

Interviewers: Turning again to *By Grand Central Station,* your attitude toward God and religion in that book is rather interesting, if not despairing. Has your attitude changed since then?

Smart: I think convenient words such as God and religion are overused now. Words such as love have lost their impact, their meaning, because they've been said over and over again. There was a time when those words were sacred, when you just didn't chat about those things but held them in a sort of reverence—at a distance beyond the commonplace. Yet, you can still give the experiences behind those words meaning by attaching events, actions and feelings to them.

Interviewers: You talked once about how it was a natural feeling for you when you were in love to want to have a child.

Smart: Yes. I think I'd be shot down by the feminists today for holding such a view. I think that deeply, basically, it is part of the sexual act to want to have a child. It doesn't happen to everybody, but when it does happen you understand it. But you don't like to say to people that they should have that feeling because then it seems to them that you are saying that they are not really in love. It is not very tactful to do this. Feminists do get a little boring and simple, you know, in their attitude to literary work. I suppose they wouldn't like my works, but I think everything is so complicated and why try to make less of it than it is?

Interviewers: It's an interesting tension. On the one hand you wrote about and lived out the "romantic" experience of being totally engrossed in love and on the other hand made it on your own as a single parent and a working woman.

Smart: But I don't think that *By Grand Central Station* is romantic. I would obstreperously deny that it is romantic. It *is* realistic. You get into a state where you fall in love and I'm not saying it was a good state or a bad state, but I just wanted to describe how it was, and I think I did that. The fact that I was madly in love with the English language and with poetry may have given vent to my feelings. George Barker has said that *By Grand Central Station* had nothing to do with him but was more a description of my love affair with the English language. I was always more interested in poetry than in other forms of literature. I'm not a novelist. I was always only interested in poetry. I was fond of the bookshops in London and in those War days the little magazines sold in those shops were big news. There was *Twentieth Century Verse*, *Poetry London*, *Horizon*, which started during the War, and *New Verse*. George Barker and Dylan Thomas first appeared in those little magazines. That's how I discovered those poets and then went out and bought their books. The London pubs were great places for literary activity. Everyone gathered at the various places to talk and drink. Women sort of kept back on the edge of the crowd as the men discussed all the exciting things that were happening.

Interviewers: Do you see correspondences now between your writing and that of Canadian authors from the same period?

Smart: Of course, I wasn't influenced by them because I wasn't in the country, but I do see some correspondences. Maybe it is something to do with being Canadian—it is very mysterious. But in general, one's own work is something for scholars to analyze.

Interviewers: Do you think that the fact you are a contemporary of Canadian writers such as Sheila Watson and Dorothy Livesay...

Smart: Oh yes, I think that has something to do with the correspondences, the fact that we are contemporaries. They are only a few years younger and older than I am, respectively, but you know Dorothy Livesay is very different from me in that she got involved in a lot of political activity and I always thought politics was nonsense. In fact, I've always found all politics extremely boring.

Interviewers: Do you have any particular favourite place in Canada?

Smart: I'm not sure, but I do find that here in Toronto there's an awful lot of creative energy. Things are happening here. The people in the street seem so full of energy. There's a lot of stuff going on on the West Coast but it is a bit sloppier. Toronto has a lot of cafés, restaurants and pubs where people can just meet and talk. This is vital if any city is to be a literary centre. There's a centre, a kind of Soho...

Interviewers: Wasn't it the British poetry editor Tambimuttu who coined the phrase "Sohoitis"?

Smart: He was very bright. He thinks he also coined the phrase "Fitzrovia" but that's inaccurate. "Fitzrovia" was the generation before ours with Augustus John and Lena Hammond and they used to go to a pub called the Fitzroy which is slightly north of Oxford Street in London. The pubs we went to in 1943 were ones like... well, we'd start at "The Black Forest" slightly over from Oxford Street and we'd wind up down at "The French" in Dean Street, which was really called "The Free French". It used to be called "The French" by the old hands but it was really "The Yorkminster". But now, much to the disgust of the old hands, it's called "The French House". The Free French used to hang out there during the War and that's why it was called "The Free French". But now, of course, everyone refers to it as "The Yorkminster". (Laughter.)

Interviewers: In your book of poetry, *A Bonus*, you wrote a poem called "Little Magazines". You've mentioned what your favourite poetry magazines were from the forties and you spoke of *Poetry London* edited by Tambimuttu.

Smart: Yes. He just died, poor soul.

Interviewers: He did another *Poetry London* just a few years ago.

Smart: That's right, and when he was in New York he did *Poetry London (New York)* and then came back to London to try to get in with the Beatles and just ended up lying in bed smoking pot and drinking beer. He never really got around to doing much. He gathered money and then frittered it away.

Interviewers: Didn't he have a hand in publishing *By Grand Central Station?*

Smart: He was entirely responsible for publishing it through Poetry London Editions. He got someone to illustrate it. But it went on for five years and nothing happened. So, finally someone else wanted to publish it. Tambi was very cross that I went with somebody else. There was an exchange of solicitors' letters, but in the end he couldn't do anything about it. There was no formal contract with Tambi. He just took me out to lunch one day and when he thought I'd had enough to drink he asked if I approved of him publishing the book and I said, "Yes it's all yours." That wouldn't hold up in a court of law.

Interviewers: During the Thirties and Forties when you were in London you went to quite a few famous literary parties. Stephen Spender described it as the "great age of hosts and hostesses."

Smart: Edmonton could do with a good hostess. (Laughter.)

Interviewers: Eddie Linden, the British poet and editor, appears in your poem "Little Magazines." How did you first encounter Eddie Linden?

Smart: I don't remember. He just seems to be an element of life. I suppose it's like asking when I encountered my first thunderstorm. (Laughter.) My son Sebastian wrote a book about him, *Who Is Eddie Linden?* and Eddie is absolutely sure now that he wrote the book himself!

Interviewers: Could you discuss your involvement in the Poetry Olympics in England, organized by Michael Horovitz?

Smart: There were thousands of us involved. A Russian read for two and a half hours. Many people walked out. He read in Russian and was translated by Frances Horovitz who did it very well—but two and a half hours! R.D. Laing also read but he got so drunk that he was booed off. There were all sorts of marvellous poets there—David Gascoyne among others.

Interviewers: What is the essential prerequisite for good writing? For you, it appears it involves having the ability to transform your own personal suffering...

Smart: I think the best person to quote on that is Proust. He wrote a wonderful thing in the very last volume of *Remembrance of Things Past*—that "suffering is a mistress I cannot deny." No matter how beautiful a girl is, it is the suffering she gives you which is valuable. And I agree. We're all so lazy that we don't even think much if we don't have to. I think suffering is the only thing that teaches anybody. You have to suffer to learn anything. I don't think you can get away with anything else, and quite rightly.

Meyer and O'Riordan

The Interviewers

Bruce Meyer was born in Toronto in 1957, and received his M.A. in English from the University of Toronto. He has held editorial posts with *Acta Victoriana*, the *University of Toronto Review*, *Descant*, *Poetry Canada Review*, *Argo* (UK), and guest-edited a special Canadian poetry issue of the *Greenfield Review* (US). He was winner of the 1980 and 1981 E.J. Pratt Gold Medals for Poetry and the 1981 and 1982 Alta Lind Cook Awards for Writing. His poems, articles and reviews have appeared internationally and he has taught at the University of Toronto.

Brian O'Riordan was born in Dublin in 1953 and received his M.A. in English from the University of Toronto, where he served on the Governing Council and was a Moss Scholar in 1980. He is currently a co-editor of *Descant* and works as a research officer for the Ontario Council on University Affairs.

Selected Bibliography

Irving Layton

Poetry

Here and Now (1945)
Cerberus (1952, with Louis Dudek and Raymond Souster)
The Improved Binoculars (1956)
A Red Carpet for the Sun (1959)
Balls for a One-Armed Juggler (1963)
The Laughing Rooster (1964)
Collected Poems (1965)
Periods of the Moon (1967)
The Shattered Plinths (1968)
Selected Poems (1969)
Nail Polish (1971)
The Collected Poems of Irving Layton (1971)
Lovers and Lesser Men (1973)
The Pole Vaulter (1974)
The Darkening Fire: Selected Poems 1945-1968
The Unwavering Eye: Selected Poems 1969-1975
For My Brother Jesus (1976)
The Covenant (1977)
The Tightrope Dancer (1978)
Droppings from Heaven (1979)
For My Neighbours in Hell (1980)
Europe and Other Bad News (1981)
A Wild and Peculiar Joy (1982)
The Gucci Bag (1983)

Other works

Canadian Poems: 1850-1952 (with Louis Dudek)
Love Where the Nights Are Long: Canadian Love Poems (1962)
Taking Sides (1977)
An Unlikely Affair (1980)

Leonard Cohen

Poetry

Let Us Compare Mythologies
(1956)
The Spice Box of Earth (1961)
Flowers for Hitler (1964)
Parasites of Heaven (1966)
Selected Poems: 1956-1968
The Energy of Slaves (1972)
Death of a Lady's Man (1978)
A Book of Mercy (prose poems/
meditations, 1984)

Novels

The Favourite Game (1963)
Beautiful Losers (1966)

Recordings

Songs of Leonard Cohen (1968)
Songs from a Room (1969)
Songs of Love and Hate (1971)
Live Songs (1973)
New Skin for the Old Ceremony
(1974)
Death of a Lady's Man (1977)
Recent Songs (1979)

Timothy Findley

Novels

The Last of the Crazy People
(1967)
The Butterfly Plague (1969)
The Wars (1977)
Famous Last Words (1981)
Not Wanted on the Voyage (1984)

Short Fiction

Dinner Along the Amazon (1984)

Plays

Can You See Me Yet? (1977)

James Reaney

Poetry

The Red Heart (1949)
A Suit of Nettles (1958)
Twelve Letters to a Small Town (1962)
The Dance of Death at London, Ontario (1963)
Poems (1972)
Selected Shorter Poems (1975)
Selected Longer Poems (1975)

Plays

The Killdeer and other plays (1962)
Colours in the Dark (1969)
Listen to the Wind (1972)
Masks of Childhood (1972)
Names and Nicknames (1972)

Apple Butter and Other Plays for Children (1973)
Sticks and Stones (1975)
St. Nicholas Hotel, Wm. Donnelly Prop. (1976)
Baldoon (with C.H. Gervais, 1976)
Handcuffs (1977)
Ignoramus (1978)
Geography (1978)
Match (1978)
Wacousta! (1979)
The Shivaree (1982)

Other Works

The Boy with an R in His Hand (1965)
14 Barrels from Sea to Sea (1977)

Dorothy Livesay

Poetry

Green Pitcher (1928)
Signpost (1932)
Day and Night (1944)
Poems for People (1947)
Call My People Home (1950)
Selected Poems (1957)
The Unquiet Bed (1967)

Collected Poems: The Two Seasons (1972)
Ice Age (1975)
The Woman I Am (1977)
Phases of Love (1983)

Other Works

Right Hand Left Hand (1977)

Raymond Souster

Poetry

Unit of Five (Edited by Ronald Hambleton, 1944)
When We Are Young (1946)
Go to Sleep World (1947)
City Hall Street (1951)
Cerberus (with Louis Dudek and Irving Layton, 1952)
Shake Hands with the Hangman (1953)
Place of Meeting (1962)
The Colour of the Times (1964)
Ten Elephants on Yonge Street (1965)
As Is (1967)
Lost & Found (1968)
So Far, So Good (1969)
The Years (1971)

Selected Poems of Raymond Souster (1972)
Charge-Up (1974)
Double Header (1975)
Rain-check (1975)
Extra Innings (1977)
Hanging In (1979)
Collected Poems (5 vols. 1980, 1981, 1982, 1983, 1984)

Other Works

Winter of Time (under pseudonym Raymond Holmes, 1949)
100 Poems of Nineteenth-Century Canada (1974)
These Loved, These Hated Lands (1975)

Gwendolyn MacEwen

Poetry

The Drunken Clock (1961)
The Rising Fire (1963)
A Breakfast for Barbarians (1966)
The Shadow-maker (1969)
The Armies of the Moon (1972)
Magic Animals (1975)
The Fire Eaters (1976)
The T.E. Lawrence Poems (1982)
Earthlight (1982)

Other works

Julian the Magician (1963)
King of Egypt, King of Dreams (1971)
Noman (1972)
Mermaids and Ikons: A Greek Summer (1978)
The Chocolate Moose (1979)
The Trojan Women (1981)
The Honey Drum (1983)

Eli Mandel

Poetry
Trio (with Phyllis Webb and Gael
    Turnbull, 1954)
Fuseli Poems (1960)
Black and Secret Man (1964)
An Idiot Joy (1967)
Stony Plain (1973)
Crusoe (1973)
Out of Place (1977)
Life Sentence (1981)
Dreaming Backwards (1983)

Other works
Five Modern Canadian Poets
    (1970)
Contexts of Canadian Criticism
    (1971)
Eight More Canadian Poets
    (1972)
Poets of Contemporary Canada
    (1972)

Milton Acorn

Poetry
In Love and Anger (1956)
The Brain's the Target (1960)
Jawbreakers (1963)
I've Tasted My Blood (1969)
More Poems for People (1972)

The Island Means Minago (1975)
Jackpine Sonnets (1977)
Captain Neal MacDougall and
    the Naked Goddess (1982)
Dig Up My Heart (1983)

Al Purdy

Poetry
The Enchanted Echo (1944)
Pressed On Sand (1955)
Emu, Remember (1956)
The Crafte So Longe to Lerne
    (1959)
Poems for All the Annettes (1962)
The Cariboo Horses (1965)
North of Summer (with A.Y.
    Jackson, 1967)
Wild Grape Wine (1968)
Love In a Burning Building (1970)
Selected Poems (1972)
Sex and Death (1973)

In Search of Owen Roblin (1974)
Sundance At Dusk (1976)
Handful of Earth (1977)
Being Alive: Poems 1958-1978
    (1978)
The Stone Bird (1981)
Bursting Into Song (1982)

Other works
Storm Warning (1971)
Al Purdy's Ontario (recording,
    1974)
Storm Warning II (1976)
No Other Country (1977)

Roo Borson

Poetry
Landfall (1977)
In the Smoky Light of the Fields
   (1980)
Rain (1980)
A Sad Device (1981)

Sheila Watson

Fiction
The Double Hook (1959)
Four Stories (1979)

Brian Moore

Fiction
The Lonely Passion of Judith
   Hearne (1955)
The Feast of Lupercal (1957)
The Luck of Ginger Coffey (1960)
An Answer from Limbo (1963)
The Emperor of Ice-cream (1965)
I Am Mary Dunne (1968)
Fergus (1970)
Catholics (1972)

The Great Victorian Collection
   (1975)
The Doctor's Wife (1976)
The Mangan Inheritance (1979)
The Temptation of Eileen
   Hughes (1981)
Cold Heaven (1983)

Other works
The Revolution Script (1971)

Elizabeth Smart

Fiction
By Grand Central Station I Sat
   Down and Wept (1945)
The Assumption of the Rogues
   and Rascals (1978)

Poetry
A Bonus (1977)
Eleven Poems (1982)

Index

Selected Titles
from
Anansi

Margaret Atwood, The Circle Game (poems)
Margaret Atwood, Power Politics (poems)
Margaret Atwood, Second Words: Selected Critical Prose
Margaret Atwood, Survival: A Thematic Guide to Canadian Literature
A.E. & C.N. Davidson, The Art of Margaret Atwood: Essays in Criticism
Don Domanski, War in an Empty House (poems)
Jacques Ferron, Selected Tales of Jacques Ferron (Translated from the
    French by Betty Bednarski)
Marian Fowler, The Embroidered Tent: Five Gentlewomen in Early
    Canada
Marian Fowler, Redney: A Life of Sara Jeannette Duncan
Northrop Frye, The Bush Garden: Essays on the Canadian Imagination
Northrop Frye, Divisions on a Ground: Essays on Canadian Culture
Graeme Gibson, Eleven Canadian Novelists (interviews)
Dennis Lee, Civil Elegies and Other Poems
Dennis Lee, Savage Fields: An Essay in Literature and Cosmology
Gwendolyn MacEwen, Mermaids & Ikons: A Greek Summer
Eli Mandel, Crusoe: Poems Selected and New
Erin Mouré, Wanted Alive (poems)
Ken Norris, ed., Canadian Poetry Now: 20 Poets of the '80's
Michael Ondaatje, The Collected Works of Billy the Kid
Michael Ondaatje, Coming Through Slaughter
Robinson & Smith, Practical Handbook of Quebec and Acadian French
Charles Taylor, Six Journeys: A Canadian Pattern (biographies)

*Anansi books are available from good booksellers across North America. Write for our
full catalogue: Anansi Press, 35 Britain Street, Toronto, Ontario M5A 1R7,
Canada.*